THE WINDING STAIRCASE

THE WINDING STAIRCASE

A VISUAL JOURNEY THROUGH
THE HISTORY AND SYMBOLISM OF THE
CRAFT AND ROYAL ARCH DEGREES

HUW PRITCHARD

This impression 2014

ISBN 978 0 85318 495 9

Published by Lewis Masonic
an imprint of Ian Allan Publishing Ltd, Hersham, Surrey KT12 4RG.

Printed in Wales

Visit the Lewis Masonic website at www.lewismasonic.co.uk

CONTENTS

ACKNOWLEDGEMENTS

I should like to thank all the staff at Lewis Masonic, most especially Pip Faulks, for their unwavering support and encouragement, likewise the teaching staff at Christie's Education in London, in particular Rebecca Lyons and Andrew Spira. I owe a debt of gratitude to my proof readers, Stephanie Clay and Kathleen Tyson Quah for their patience, understanding and unwavering accuracy; any remaining typographical errors are mine and mine alone. I must also thank Martin Cherry at the Library and Museum of Freemasonry in London and Terence Haunch for their assistance and interest and for their permission to use many of the photographs in this book. I am grateful to the members of the Old Epsomian Lodge No.3561 and the Surrey Schools Chapter No.3561 for their fraternal friendship over the past thirty years or so. Lastly, I should like to thank my wife Lorraine and my children Siobhan and Tom who have encouraged and supported me through my own challenging journey.

This book is dedicated to my parents John Pritchard (1926-1995) and Lois Pritchard (1929-2012).

Introduction

Freemasonry is one of the World's oldest secular associations with its modern origins dating to the remnants of the medieval stonemasons' guilds operating in the late seventeenth century. Today it is one of the largest fraternal societies in the world; it promotes high levels of moral conduct and integrity in its members and is a major contributor to charities, both Masonic and non-Masonic. In the past, over-zealous notions of privacy created an impression of secrecy and mystery, which led to misplaced accusations of corruption and improper behaviour by its members. The resulting and very welcome official policy of openness and transparency has led to a wider understanding of its aims and ideals. One of the most important aspects of Freemasonry is to provide its members with tools to enable them to embark on a voyage of self-discovery and self-improvement, ultimately assisting them to gain a better understanding of their own spirituality.

There can be few non-fictional organisations which have generated as much imaginative speculation about their aims, purpose and origins than Freemasonry. It is at once mysterious and intriguing and certainly provides ample source material for both the conspiracy theorist and the novelist. Dan Brown famously makes use of explicitly Masonic themes in *The Last Symbol* whilst Stephen Knight in *Jack the Ripper: The Final Solution* even suggests that the Jack the Ripper murders in Whitechapel in 1888 were the result of a conspiracy between the Freemasons and the Royal Family. Even within Masonic circles there are plenty of controversial, if perhaps slightly less colourful theories surrounding the origins of Freemasonry. There are books suggesting that it developed from the practices of the Knights Templar, dating back to the early days of the Crusaders in Jerusalem, whilst other writers have linked Freemasonry to the Mithraic cults of the classical world and even ancient Egypt.

Sensational publications about Freemasonry are nothing new, as the earliest Masonic exposés appeared shortly after the founding of the first Grand Lodge in 1717. However, for a reportedly 'secret' society English Freemasonry is remarkably open: its headquarters at Freemasons' Hall in London is open to the public, offering regular (and free) guided tours. Researchers both Masonic and non-Masonic are welcomed in its library, and its rules and regulations and indeed a wealth of Masonic books are freely available to the general public.

Although there are both female and mixed-sex Masonic orders in existence, Freemasonry in England is overwhelmingly male. According to the United Grand Lodge of England there are about a quarter of a million Freemasons in England and Wales and around 150,000 in the whole of Scotland and Ireland, both of which are administered by their own Grand Lodges. For many of its members Freemasonry is simply an enjoyable hobby in a pleasant environment and perhaps a way of making new friends. Undoubtedly it also provides a focus for charitable activities: for example, one of the four major Masonic charities, The Freemasons' Grand Charity (founded 1980), has donated more than 100 million pounds to a wide range of charitable causes since its inception, while many other non-Masonic charities have received support from individual Freemasons, their lodges and their Provincial or Metropolitan Grand Lodges.

What makes Freemasonry different from Round Table or Rotary clubs are its rituals and ceremonies. All Freemasons, almost by definition, enjoy this aspect of the Craft of Freemasonry and find participation in the ceremonies to be a deeply enjoyable and satisfying experience. The rituals can be enjoyed on many levels; certainly, the degree ceremonies all contain significant lessons about morality, which stress the importance of living moral and upright lives but also place significant emphasis on maintaining harmony, both within the lodge and Society, as a whole. However, for the more thoughtful and perhaps more curious Freemason there are deeper lessons to be drawn from Masonic ritual, which for some are profoundly spiritual. As well as undertaking a journey of self-discovery, the Freemason may also gain a far deeper understanding of his own spiritual beliefs.

The progression of a Freemason through the different degrees of Freemasonry is often described as a journey but it is also, perhaps less obviously, one in which Freemasonry's own development may be traced. The rituals and ceremonies of Freemasonry, or perhaps the manner in which Masonic symbolism and allegory is presented to its members, did not suddenly appear fully formed at the end of the seventeenth century when it seems that non-stonemasons first began to join operative stonemasons' lodges. As Freemasonry began to be become more widespread, both as a fashionable pastime for the wealthy and aristocratic and as an intellectual pursuit enjoyed by leading thinkers of the early eighteenth century, so the rituals and the symbolism used by Freemasons' lodges began to take shape. Although some very old Masonic ritual practices, such as the Baldwyn Rite in Bristol, do still survive, almost all current forms of Masonic ritual throughout England and Wales date back to the Lodges of Reconciliation established after the Union of the two main Grand Lodges in 1813. By examining the development and use of Masonic symbols and imagery, and in particular by looking at specific objects which relate to Masonic ritual, it is also possible to gain some understanding of how speculative Freemasonry evolved from its earliest beginnings in the medieval guilds of stonemasons into the secular fraternity it is today.

As well as examining objects, which feature in Craft Freemasonry this book also looks at objects relating to the degree of the Holy Royal Arch of Jerusalem, probably the most commonly encountered of all 'side' degrees. Long described as a completion of the third degree in Freemasonry, that of the Master Mason, it is now recognised as a separate degree in its own right; its previous description was almost certainly a compromise between the two rival Grand Lodges as they moved towards union. What is certain is that it is widely understood to be the culmination of the three Craft degrees, which is why United Grand Lodge today urges all Craft Freemasons to join a Royal Arch chapter.

Far from being a murky secret society, there is a wealth of literature explaining how Freemasonry uses its symbols and imagery to illuminate the path of self-discovery trodden by the thoughtful Freemason. Indeed, it is Freemasonry's use of symbolism and allegory, which provides the Freemason with tools to assist him in facing the challenges of both his everyday life and his spirituality. The aim of this book is twofold: by looking at objects used directly and indirectly in Masonic ritual it aims to shed some light on both the development of English Freemasonry itself and on the modern day Freemason's journey of self-discovery.

ONE

The Evolution of Speculative Freemasonry in England and the Establishment of Grand Lodge

Over the years, there have been a great many theories about the origins of Freemasonry. Some writers have linked its genesis and traditions to the medieval chivalric order of the Knights Templar: indeed, there is even a Masonic order of Knights Templar, although this certainly has no direct link at all with the original order but is rather a nineteenth-century revival. Almost all of these theories probably owe rather more to the imagination and to wishful thinking than to historical documentation or even evidence from its artistic history. It seems most likely that 'speculative' Freemasonry (as opposed to operative masonry practised by stonemasons) largely developed first in England, although its rapid spread to continental Europe and beyond provided many opportunities for English Freemasonry both to influence and be influenced by other Masonic traditions. Scottish Freemasonry, in particular, has developed along a separate path for much of its existence and has its own customs, however there is no doubt that the first Grand Lodge to exist in Freemasonry was founded in London in 1717 and it is from London that modern English Freemasonry traces its descent. There have been other English Grand Lodges outside of London, most notably the Grand Lodge of All England based in York and its daughter Grand Lodge, the Grand Lodge of England South of the River Trent, which certainly played a part in the development of English Freemasonry; however these Grand Lodges have not persisted, and London was unquestionably the birthplace of the Craft as it is practised in England today.

Some of the main sources of evidence for the development of non-operative or speculative Freemasonry are the illustrated exposés and satirical prints, published mainly in the eighteenth century, and the later survivals of ritual objects, especially the ritual images once painted on floorcloths but now known as 'tracing boards'. The latter in particular provide a fascinating insight into the development of Masonic ritual from its earliest forms, which appear to have been based on a catechism, to the ritual dramas familiar to Freemasons today.

Whilst most authorities agree that the distant origins of Freemasonry almost certainly lie with the medieval guilds of masons who built the cathedrals of northern Europe, the actual development of non-operative or speculative ritual procedure is less clear. The earliest surviving evidence of non-operative Freemasonry dates back only to the seventeenth century and, even then, evidence is somewhat scarce. It also seems very likely that modern Masonic ritual did not evolve gradually from the practices of the medieval guilds but instead developed quite rapidly in the early years of the eighteenth century and is perhaps more rooted in the Enlightenment than in the Middle Ages.

Medieval stonemasons were by their nature peripatetic in that they travelled to the site of their work and then tended to stay there for the duration of the construction. It is also quite likely that they formed their own communities on the site of the new building rather than integrating into the local community, as happened in the eighteenth and nineteenth centuries when armies of Irish 'navvies' built first the canal system and later the railway networks. It has been suggested that one of the possible origins of the term 'freemason' comes from this ability to move to different sites rather than being fixed at one location. However, it is just as likely that the term 'free' actually derives from 'freestone mason' (such stones were fine-grained and more easily carved) or from 'free' in the sense of being a higher calibre of craftsman who has served his apprenticeship and is no longer indentured to his Master.

Medieval stonemasons, as with many other trades, normally served an apprenticeship of at least seven years. Initially they would be taken on as entered apprentices and in due time would progress to the level of fellow craftsmen or journeymen. The term 'journeyman' derives from the French *journée* meaning 'day', as a journeyman had the right to be paid by the day although, as he was not yet a 'Master', he could not employ other workmen. Each stage of his apprenticeship would be marked with oaths to keep secret not only the guild's working practices but also the signs and passwords of his new rank. When seeking work on a new site these signs and passwords would serve not so much to prove his competence, which could easily be tested by a practical examination, but to show that he had been pledged formally into the craft and was aware of its customs and requirements. These rites of progression would also be marked by the recital of the traditional history of the craft and by an exhortation to high standards of moral conduct. In due course, this exhortation was formalised into what became known as the Old Charges. A version of the Old Charges, which in their earliest written form appear to date back to the late fourteenth century, is still read out to the Master-elect at the annual lodge meeting when the new Master is installed into the chair of his lodge.

In time, the guilds became part of the fabric of society: their members were often the same people who ran the municipalities at a local level. Indeed, remnants of similar survivals can still be seen today in, for example, the livery companies of the Corporation of the City of London. In addition, it can be argued that just like today, membership could provide a focus for charitable work, whilst the social side of guild membership, essentially drinking and feasting, was an important way of demonstrating high social standing.

One of the earliest recorded initiations of a non-operative Freemason into a stonemasons' lodge was that of the founder of the Ashmolean Museum in Oxford, Elias Ashmole

(1617-1692), who was initiated into a lodge in Warrington on 16 October 1646. In his journal, Ashmole names the existing members of the lodge he joined, none of whom was an operative stonemason. Although the traditional view of earlier Masonic historians was that modern speculative Freemasonry developed gradually from the workings of operative stonemasons' lodges, more modern Masonic historians convincingly argue that much of the evidence in favour of this relies on quite a small number of historical sources, including Ashmole's journal and other works written by those who can be said to have had a connection with Ashmole, all of whom had alchemical and esoteric interests. It should be remembered that modern divisions between science and what we might today term pseudo-science and what was then called alchemy simply did not exist in the seventeenth century: it is now known, for example, that Sir Isaac Newton had a deep and long-lasting interest in alchemy. In any case, there is very little evidence to clearly suggest that the development of speculative Freemasonry was at all widespread during the late seventeenth and very early eighteenth centuries, especially when compared to the much more compelling evidence of speculative Masonic working, which started to appear from the 1730s.

In the early years of the eighteenth century, London Freemasonry was in most respects moribund: the 1734 re-print of James Anderson's *Constitutions* refers to the 'drooping lodges of London' of the past, and the later 1738 edition notes that 'in the South the lodges were more and more disused'. This situation changed enormously after the first or Premier Grand Lodge was founded in London in June 1717 by four London lodges at the Goose and Gridiron Ale-house in St. Paul's Churchyard. Its foundation marks the start of a period of rapid growth and radical development in speculative Freemasonry, particularly following the installation of the third Grand Master, John Theophilus Desaguliers (1683-1744) in 1719. Desaguliers, a Huguenot clergyman, was a Fellow of the Royal Society and appears to have stimulated great interest in Freemasonry in other members of the intellectual community. While the influx of highly educated and intelligent new members was to provide the future intellectual backbone of speculative Freemasonry, just as importantly it was the installation of an aristocratic Grand Master, the 2nd Duke of Montagu (also a Fellow of the Royal Society), in 1721, that made Freemasonry fashionable and caused the number of lodges to grow rapidly. By 1725, just eight years after the foundation of the Premier Grand Lodge, the number of lodges under its jurisdiction had grown from four to sixty and by 1730, there were over a hundred.

The newly fashionable status of Freemasonry created its own problems, not least a huge increase in public interest. The publication in 1730 of Samuel Prichard's *Masonry*

Dissected, which ran through three editions in eleven days, was simply the first of many exposés of what really was at that time a secretive organisation. Despite the sensationalist nature of some of the exposés, it is accepted that some of them, such as *Masonry Dissected*, are probably quite accurate portrayals of what went on in eighteenth-century lodge rooms and, given the prohibition against writing down any of the ritual, some copies may well have been purchased by Freemasons seeking a better understanding of their Craft.

Most early eighteenth-century lodges met in inns and ale-houses and had a reputation for drunkenness, although in early eighteenth-century London such behaviour was hardly exceptional. The publication and adoption of James Anderson's (c.1679-1739) *The Constitutions of the Free-Masons* in 1723 may have provided a firm and lasting foundation for Grand Lodge, but it is probably the case that some members saw this as interfering with the rather genial nature of their social dining and drinking club. Matters came to a head in 1724 when the second Duke of Montagu's successor as Grand Master, Philip Wharton, 1st Duke of Wharton (1698-1731), a past-president of the notorious Hellfire Club, was defeated in the following year's election for Grand Master by just one vote. Wharton took this defeat very badly and threatened to withdraw all his supporters from Grand Lodge. It is possible that Wharton may have considered setting up a new order, the Gormagons, to rival Grand Lodge, although it is more likely that the Gormagons were a hoax perpetrated by Montagu's faction in an attempt to discredit any attempt by Wharton's faction to establish such an order. William Hogarth (1685-1764) took advantage of the situation to publish his print, *Masonry brought to light by the Gormagons* (**Fig.1**).

Although Hogarth had not yet been initiated into Freemasonry at the time of its publication, he was clearly aware of Masonic symbolism. Freemasonry itself is represented as an old woman seated on a donkey; the Duke of Wharton is shown dressed as Don Quixote in armour with a shield and a feather on his helmet directing the procession: his stance and armour refer to a popular contemporary print of Don Quixote by Charles-Antoine Coypel (1694-1752). The monkey, clothed in an apron and gloves, is a reference to the fictitious Gormagons' attempt to 'ape' Freemasonry, while the figure in the apron with his head poking through the ladder is James Anderson.

In spite of the ridicule he poured on aspects of Freemasonry in the *Gormagons* print, William Hogarth was himself initiated into Freemasonry during 1725. He was a member of the lodge which met at the Hand and Apple Tree tavern in Little Great Street, Holborn, which was consecrated in November 1725. Hogarth's father-in-law, Sir James Thornhill (1675-1734), was both a Fellow of the Royal Society and a Freemason of some note:

ABOVE **Fig.1: William Hogarth's satirical print, The Mystery of Masonry brought to light by the Gormagons, 1724.** *Image © The Library and Museum of Freemasonry, London.*

Thornhill attained the high Masonic rank of Senior Grand Warden in 1728 while Hogarth achieved the lesser rank of Grand Steward in 1735. Hogarth later designed the Grand Steward's jewel, which was worn by Grand Stewards as part of their regalia until it was superseded by a new centenary jewel in 1835.

Probably Hogarth's most famous depiction of Freemasonry appears in his series of paintings entitled *The Four Times of Day* (1736-38) which were made into a very popular series of prints in 1738. The fourth scene, *Night* (**Fig.2**), shows a typically Hogarthian scene of chaos, mayhem and disorder. Whilst it focuses on a drunken Freemason wearing his Master's collar with the Set Square jewel, who is being escorted home by a servant and unfortunately drenched by the contents of a chamber-pot flung from one of the upper-storey windows, other small vignettes of eighteenth-century London life crowd the frame, from the overturned carriage to the open window where a rather worried-looking man is being shaved.

NIGHT

Even though it is certainly true that Freemasons' lodges had a reputation for drinking and drunkenness, which is being satirised, in *Night* it seems that there may be a more personal aspect to this portrayal: the drunken Freemason has been traditionally identified as the Magistrate Sir Thomas de Veil. It is known that in 1736, both Hogarth and de Veil were members of the lodge which met at the Vine Tavern in Holborn, and it appears that there was a degree of animosity between them. In any case, Sir Thomas de Veil was well known for his involvement in official attempts to restrict the illegal production of gin, the vast consumption of which was having a calamitous effect on the public, and for his prosecution of illegal gin houses: by portraying him as a drunkard, Hogarth is accusing him of hypocrisy. Masonic historians have suggested that the painting may also refer to a well-known occasion when Sir Thomas de Veil had accidentally swallowed a draught of urine when testing a bottle of suspected illegal gin. Sir Thomas de Veil's escort has been identified as the Grand Tyler, Andrew Montgomery.

A far more significant split than Wharton's took place in 1751 with the formation of a rival Grand Lodge which deemed itself to be more in keeping with older traditions. This newer body took to describing itself as the 'Antients' whilst referring to the original, Premier Grand Lodge, somewhat confusingly, as the 'Moderns'. In part, at least, the cause of the split can be traced back to Prichard's exposé *Masonry Dissected*: in order to prevent non-Masons spuriously gaining access to lodge meetings, the Premier Grand Lodge reversed the passwords of the first two degrees in Freemasonry. One major effect of this was that many Irish Freemasons who had been initiated in Irish lodges were now unable to gain access to their local lodges in London and so formed their own Grand Lodge.

The newer Grand Lodge, the 'Antients', claimed that they alone worked 'Pure Antient Masonry' and disliked what they saw as the unnecessary, improper and 'modern' innovations of the Premier Grand Lodge. The two rival Grand Lodges co-existed, neither one recognising the other, for more than sixty years until, after four years of negotiations, the two rival Grand Lodges finally agreed to merge in December 1813.

The Union would have a profound effect on Masonic ritual and imagery, which stabilised, with a few subsequent changes, into the forms used today. However, it is arguably the period of the two Grand Lodges which saw the greatest changes in Masonic working practices, much of which can be seen in the use and development of the ritual images known as

LEFT **Fig.2: William Hogarth's satirical print, The Four Times of Day, Night, 1738.**

Image © The Library and Museum of Freemasonry, London.

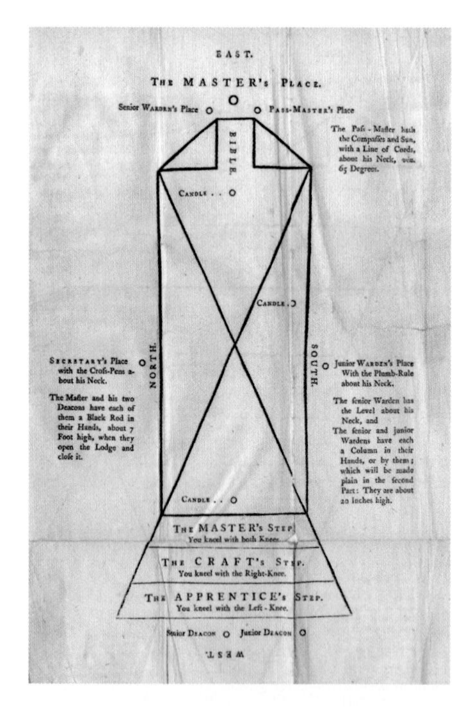

ABOVE **Fig. 3: Drawing from the Masonic exposé Three distinct knocks (1760) showing the 'drawing of the lodge'.** *Image © The Library and Museum of Freemasonry, London.*

'tracing boards'. At early lodge meetings, most of which were held in taverns, the symbols and forms of the lodge itself were marked out on the floor in chalk or charcoal and were cleaned off at the end of meetings, although it seems that some lodges may have used tapes pinned to the floor. The minute-books of lodges from the early eighteenth century have many references to 'drawing the lodge' which was usually one of the duties of the lodge's Tyler or 'outer guard', whose main duty was (and still is) to remain outside the door of the lodge room during meetings, to ensure that the meeting was not disturbed by non-members.

The 'drawing of the lodge' could be quite simple, as may be seen from a diagram published in the 1760 exposé *Three Distinct Knocks* (**Fig.3**), which claimed to reveal the working of the Antients: it shows a rectangular shape with a triangular part to the East for the Master and the Bible. A slightly later exposé, *Jachin and Boaz*, from 1762 (**Fig.4**) claiming to reveal Masonic working 'both Antient and Modern', includes a slightly more complicated plan, perhaps hinting at the increased ornamentation already finding favour with the Moderns and which the Antients found so objectionable. However, both plans are broadly rectangular with a triangular extension to the East for the Master and the Bible. It should be noted that References to the compass-points within lodge rooms are entirely figurative, the Master's place being 'in the East': Lodge rooms are not aligned with the geographical compass.

Even if the very simple plan of *Three Distinct Knocks* were used, it is clear that drawing the necessary lines each time would have been a laborious task, and even as early as 1733 there are examples of lodges resolving to have permanent plans painted onto canvas to save the trouble of drawing the lodge each time it met. This is especially true of more sophisticated lodges with a more aristocratic membership, where the very simple layouts shown in *Three Distinct Knocks* and *Jachin and Boaz* would simply not have been acceptable.

The increasing sophistication of these floor coverings may well reflect a continental influence. A French exposé from 1745 by J.M. Bernigeroth, *Les Coutumes des Francs-Maçons dans leurs Assemblées* (**Fig.5**) has seven plates showing the lodge at work with a more detailed floorcloth clearly visible. A later English exposé from 1766, *Mahabone* (**Fig.6**), has as its frontispiece a 'Drawing on the Floor of a Lodge', an elaborate image which would clearly have been difficult to draw without considerable effort.

Throughout the second half of the eighteenth century there are increasing references to painted floorcloths in lodge minutes, even if their use was not officially sanctioned. Due to their fragile nature, very few of these floorcloths have survived: *The Lodge of Hope No.433 Floorcloth*, which dates from about 1780, is a very rare example as well as being a very fine one (**Fig.7**). Although different in format, it has much in common with the frontispiece to *Mahabone* in that there is very little attempt to depict a naturalistic setting. In *Mahabone* the symbols are placed in an almost haphazard manner rather than with any great sense of aesthetic sensibility or indeed ritual significance: there is no sense of scale or coherent structure.

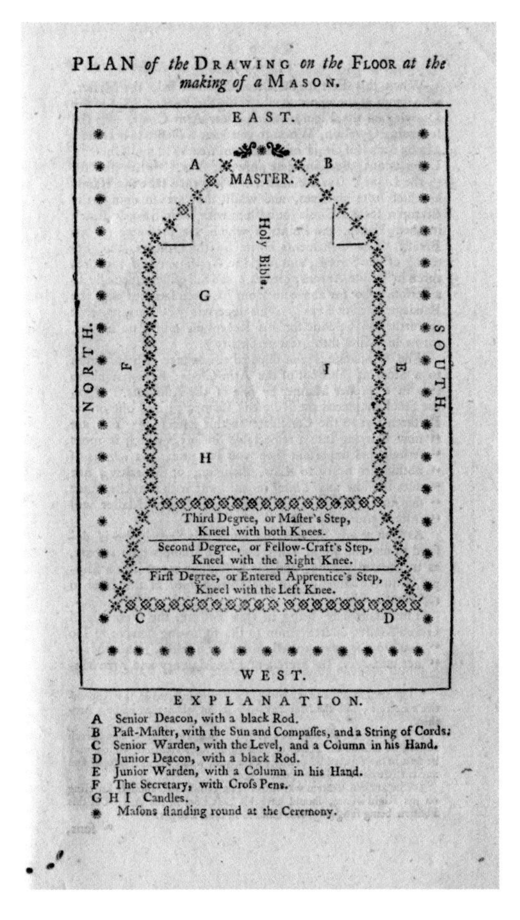

ABOVE **Fig.4: Drawing from the exposé Jachin and Boaz (1762) suggesting the more elaborate working favoured by the Moderns.** *Image © The Library and Museum of Freemasonry, London.*

ABOVE **Fig 5: An eighteenth century French print showing the initiation ceremony. Assembly of Freemasons for the Reception of Apprentices, Plate I from J.M. Bernigeroth, Les Coutumes des Francs-Maçons dans leurs Assemblées.** *Image © The Library and Museum of Freemasonry, London.*

Unlike later tracing boards, *The Lodge of Hope No.433 floorcloth* is not specific to a particular degree ceremony: it depicts a number of Masonic symbols which are not arranged in terms of their ritual importance, although the Greater and Lesser Lights (the Square and Compasses on the Volume of the Sacred Law and the Sun (which has almost completely faded away at the top left), Moon, Blazing Star and Jacob's Ladder) are placed towards the top. Even so, the symbols have been laid out thoughtfully, and even though the execution is, at best, somewhat crude, the objects have still been painted with some care; nevertheless, it retains the nature of a chart or diagram. None of the objects relate to each other spatially, neither do they share the same sense of scale: the floorcloth is essentially a list of symbols to be explained. It is a very rare survivor, as many wore out or were simply thrown away when more permanent tracing boards were acquired. During the Second World War, *The Lodge of Hope No.433 floorcloth* was stored underneath the floorboards of the Masonic Hall in Brightlingsea, having been rolled up into an iron drainpipe for safe-keeping.

Other early floorcloths do show some awareness of composition: The Lodge of Union No.129 in Kendal has a set of three floorcloths possibly dating from 1772, which still have the essential characteristics of a diagram or plan but which have also clearly been arranged into an altogether more aesthetically conscious composition (**Fig.8**). The first degree floorcloth has one step for the first degree and has a tasselled pentagonal border as found in the floor plans of the early exposés. The second degree cloth adds a second step and further symbolism, whilst the third degree cloth has a third step and adds yet more symbols, including the mosaic pavement from the inner chamber of King Solomon's Temple which later featured on first degree tracing boards. These incremental steps correspond to the 'regular steps' undertaken by the candidate in each of the degree ceremonies.

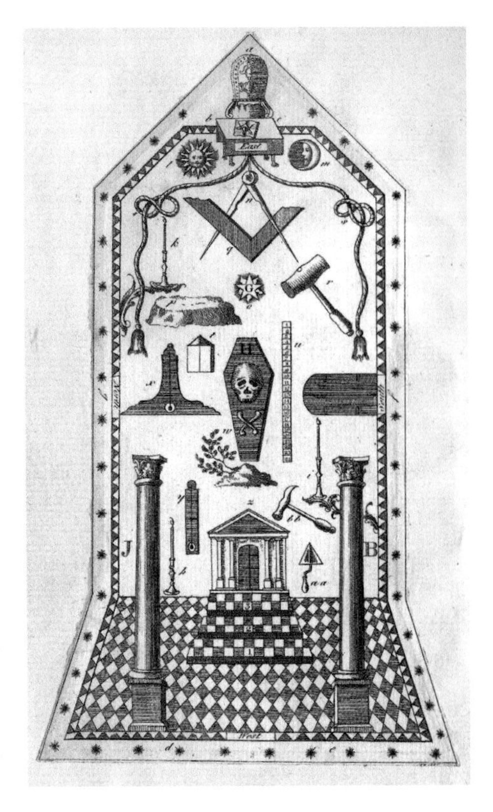

ABOVE **Fig 6: Frontispiece of Mahabone, (1766).**

Image © The Library and Museum of Freemasonry, London.

Whilst these painted floorcloths were becoming increasingly popular, especially as they could be rolled up and put away when not in use, other lodges were making boards available to their Tylers on which they could draw the necessary forms. Initially, both floorcloths and boards were placed on the floor during meetings; however, as lodges paid for painted cloths and boards of increasing complexity it seems that it became more common for them to be placed on trestles or possibly hung on the wall with rollers, as was the case with the three cloths of the Lodge of Union No.129. It is possible that the American Masonic term 'trestle boards' derives from this practice, although other variants such as 'trasel board' and the French term *planche à tracer* had been in use since the middle of the eighteenth century or even earlier, implying that perhaps 'tracing board' and 'trestle board' are both correct but derive from different

ABOVE **Fig.7: The Lodge of Hope No.433 Floorcloth, c.1780.**

Image © The Library and Museum of Freemasonry, London.

sources. Certainly there is pictorial evidence from prints showing tracing boards being supported on tables, at least in Europe.

These painted boards and cloths began to demonstrate increasing degrees of artistic sophistication. *The Tracing Board of the Lodge of Unions No.256* (**Fig.9**), made around 1801, is a notable example of this. Although in some ways its construction is rugged and primitive, its design nevertheless exhibits high levels of artistic sophistication. Even without an understanding of the Masonic symbols it displays, it remains an object of great beauty, which would arguably not look out of place in an exhibition of surrealist art with its juxtaposition of enigmatic symbols and seemingly unrelated objects of mysterious use.

The outer frame of the board is decorated with a neoclassical Greek key motif, which has no apparent ritual significance and seems purely decorative. The four tassels at the corners represent the Four Cardinal Virtues of Temperance, Fortitude, Justice and Mercy. The inner panel to the left marked 'N' stands proud of the panel on the right marked 'E','S' and 'W' as if it should slide across, however there is nothing to suggest that this has ever been the case. Even though its form is very different from modern tracing boards both panels contain symbols normally found on them today, although unusually there are no Square and Compasses resting on the Volume of the Sacred Law and neither are there representations of Faith, Hope and Charity on Jacob's Ladder. Also unusual is the depiction of the Mosaic Pavement, which includes six squares of a different colour rather than the more usual chequerboard pattern of black and white squares. The significance of the six differently coloured squares is no longer clear.

The inclusion of Euclid's 47th Proposition implies that it might have been used as a 'Master's board' during the Inner Working of the Installation ceremony as this is now used as the symbol of a Past Master. For the operative stonemason, the Pythagorean discovery that the ratio of 3:4:5 would produce a right-angle triangle was possibly the most essential secret of all: hence in speculative Freemasonry it was generally restricted to those who had been 'through the chair'. Apart from its depiction on Past Masters' collars, it no longer features in modern working.

On the left hand panel, above the Mosaic Pavement, is a representation of a Lewis, a series of metal plates which, when slotted into a suitable cavity on the top of a block of stone, would enable it to be lifted into place by a hoist or derrick. Today, the uninitiated son of a Freemason is referred to as a 'Lewis'. The floor plan within which the Lewis sits is possibly a representation of the Sanctum Sanctorum, near which was the final resting-place of Hiram Abiff according to the Hiramic legend which forms such an important part of Masonic ritual.

LEFT AND ABOVE **Fig.8: Three floor cloths, c.1772, on painted cloth belonging to The Lodge of Union No.129, Kendal.** *Photos © Terence Haunch.*

RIGHT **Fig. 9: Tracing Board of the Lodge of Unions No.256. c.1801.** *Image © The Library and Museum of Freemasonry, London.*

The unknown artist who made this tracing board has not attempted to create a naturalistic three-dimensional space as later artists did: however the balanced and elegant composition which is both full of symbolic meaning and yet remains remarkably uncluttered makes this tracing

board succeed both as a ritual object and as a fascinating work of art. It is certainly not a naturalistic representation of carefully placed, symbolically significant objects such as may be found in many sixteenth- and seventeenth-century still-life paintings, especially those concerned with mortality, which are often referred to as 'Vanitas' paintings, and yet it is far more than just a diagram or list of symbols to be explained. With its direct use of symbolism and somewhat stark composition it might even be said to have more in common with works of art from the twentieth century than with those of its own period.

This increasing sophistication of tracing boards and floorcloths is a reflection of changes that were occurring in Masonic practice at the same time. Early lodge meetings were both social and ceremonial with much of the Masonic instruction based on a catechism: the questions and answers were mixed with charges and toasts whilst Masonic ceremonial itself was mainly restricted to the admission of candidates. Gradually lodge meetings separated into two parts: a ritual-based lodge meeting with ceremonies of increasing complexity followed by a meal which is still known to this day as the 'festive board'. Elements of the old practices do still survive: at Royal Arch festive boards a series of questions is posed by the First Principal (the equivalent of Worshipful Master in a Craft lodge) to an officer called the Principal Sojourner. The Craft catechisms themselves survive in the Craft *Lectures* which are still worked by private lodges, if only occasionally.

As with the floorcloths of The Lodge of Union No.129, lodges were increasingly using separate boards or floorcloths for each of the three degrees. Very early designers such as John Cole, who published a series of designs in *Illustrations of Masonry* (1801), still tended to favour very simple designs, which might perhaps best be described as charts or diagrams. However a contemporary of Cole's, John Browne, began to produce designs which were more aesthetically pleasing and even made use of colour: a departure from old practices, which were still based on the monochrome forms drawn on the floor of the lodge in chalk or charcoal (**Fig.10**).

Of the early tracing board designers, probably the most important was the portrait painter Josiah Bowring (1757-1832). Although not otherwise an artist of any great significance, his tracing board designs show a greater degree of artistic sensibility than his predecessors: indeed the noted Masonic historian Terence Haunch remarked that his designs had 'the classical simplicity, refinement and repose of the late Georgian Age'.

Bowring's design for the *First Degree Tracing Board of the Lodge of Honor and Generosity No.165* (**Fig.11**) is a much more successful composition than earlier designs with, for example, a more convincing sense of perspective: the Boards themselves become objects of contemplation rather than simply diagrams containing Masonic symbols.

In his *First Degree Tracing Board* of 1819, Bowring places the three columns, with their attributes of Wisdom, Strength and Beauty, in accordance with modern Masonic practice, within a fictive three-dimensional space, for which he has used the orthogonals of the Mosaic Pavement to provide a sense of perspective.

RIGHT **Fig.10: Printed illustrations of tracing boards for each degree designed by John Browne (also pictured) c.1800.** *Image © The Library and Museum of Freemasonry, London.*

T
G
HA
HKT
SKI
D
I
C

E
S
W

H. A
M. B
T. C
G

HZI
G
Mr. John Browne,
Editor of the General Law List, London Conductor, &c.

ABOVE **Fig.11: Josiah Bowring, First Degree Tracing Board, 1819.**

Image © The Library and Museum of Freemasonry, London.

Bowring was amongst the first to show the three Christian Virtues of Faith, Hope and Charity as female figures: Faith with a book at the bottom of the ladder, Hope with an anchor in the middle, and Charity with a small child at the top. The key hanging from the ladder has now mostly disappeared from Masonic imagery: here it seems to refer to the passwords used by Freemasons to confirm their identity. The ladder leads to the heavens represented by the Sun, the Moon with seven stars, (referring to the Seven Liberal Arts and Sciences) and the all-seeing eye of God. The seven stars may also represent the seven masons who, according to the ritual, make the lodge 'perfect'.

The first degree working-tools of the Twenty-Four Inch Gauge, Gavel and Chisel are placed on the roughly-hewn block of stone, the Rough Ashlar, towards the rear, ready to transform the uneducated newly-initiated Freemason into the useful member of society represented by the Perfect Ashlar to the right of the Ionic column. By resting these ritual objects against the columns and the Ashlars, Bowring has anchored them within the ritual space he has created: unlike earlier, more diagrammatic tracing boards, these objects relate to each other spatially, making the entire composition more aesthetically (and arguably, ritually) coherent.

The elegant simplicity of Bowring's late Regency design is in contrast to the perhaps more bombastic naturalism of John Harris's *First Degree Tracing Board* (**Fig.12**) painted for the Emulation Lodge of Improvement in 1845. This tracing board is probably more familiar to many Freemasons today due to its inclusion in modern copies of the 'blue book' of Emulation ritual, which is today possibly the most widely-used version of Masonic ritual. The capitals on the top of Harris's columns converging on the figure of Faith at the bottom of the ladder, whilst obeying the rules of perspective, appear rather top-heavy and awkward compared to Bowring's gentler, less rigorous composition.

The period from 1740 to 1800 not only saw an increase in the ritual sophistication of Craft Freemasonry but also the development of a large number of other Masonic degrees. Some of these, rather confusingly, included the word 'Scottish' or 'Ecossais' (from the French) in their names despite having little or nothing to do with Scotland itself. By the mid-1760s, a rite of twenty-five Ecossais degrees was being practised in both continental Europe and the North American states. Also known as the Ancient and Accepted Rite (or more commonly *Rose Croix* after the eighteenth degree usually worked) the Scottish Rite's ruling Supreme Council published its first constitutions around 1762. A great many other degrees were worked in one form or another, many of which fell into disuse, although there are significant numbers still operating today, all of which require at least membership of a Craft lodge as an

ABOVE **Fig.12: John Harris, First Degree Tracing Board, 1845.**

Photo © Ian Allan Publishing Ltd.

entry qualification. Probably the most important 'higher degrees' worked in the early nineteenth century were the 'Holy Royal Arch of Jerusalem' (commonly referred to as the Royal Arch) and Mark Masonry, which included the two degrees of 'Mark Man' and 'Mark Master'. Mark Masonry today operates under its own Grand Mark Lodge, whereas Royal Arch Masonry is administered by the Supreme Grand Chapter, which is constituted under the United Grand Lodge of England.

By 1813 the two rival Grand Lodges, the Antients and the Premier Grand Lodge, had been in rather fractious competition for more than sixty years. Even though they had been negotiating about the possibility of a merger for four years, it was only when the Prince Regent, later George IV, resigned as Grand Master of the Premier Grand Lodge (the 'Moderns') and was succeeded by his brother the Duke of Sussex that the merger actually took place. Undoubtedly, it helped that another royal brother, the Duke of Kent, was then Grand Master of the Antients; however, the importance of the part played by the Duke of Sussex cannot be overestimated.

Augustus, Duke of Sussex was the sixth son of King George III and was both strong-willed and somewhat unconventional. He married twice, both times in contravention of the Royal Marriages Act of 1772, which meant that as neither marriage was officially recognised he died without legitimate heirs. Having witnessed the chaotic funeral of his brother King William IV at Windsor in 1837, he left instructions that he should be buried in the large new public cemetery in Kensal Green. His second wife, Lady Cecilia Buggin, who was created Duchess of Inverness in her own right by Queen Victoria (the Duke of Sussex was reportedly Queen Victoria's favourite uncle and had lobbied vigorously on her behalf), was later interred with him. Such Royal patronage had a huge effect on the success of these new out-of-town cemeteries, built to relieve the appalling and insanitary congestion of the inner London burial-grounds.

The Duke of Sussex was without question a thoughtful and educated man: he was President of the Royal Society of Arts from 1816 until his death in 1843 and President of the Royal Society from 1830 to 1838. In its early days, the future of the United Grand Lodge of England was by no means assured and many at the time felt that the Duke of Sussex had played a central role in ensuring its success. So much so that on the twenty-fifth anniversary of the Union, and therefore his Grand-Mastership, he was presented with a very large solid-silver centrepiece weighing some 2,000 ounces, which is now held within the collection of the Library and Museum of Freemasonry. This extraordinary object is an odd and rather unhappy mixture of the rococo and neoclassical, which could only ever

have appealed to the somewhat eclectic sensibilities of early Victorian taste. It was made by the prestigious firm of R and S Garrard and Co. (**Figs 13a and 13b.**)

The most important issues facing the first Grand Master of the new United Grand Lodge concerned the Craft's attitude towards religion; the status of the 'higher degrees' and the standardisation of regalia; and (perhaps the most important issue of all) ritual. The Duke of Sussex was known to be in favour of Catholic emancipation and had many Jewish friends, and his influence was instrumental in making the new United Grand Lodge open to those of other faiths.

Before the Union, Masonic regalia had varied considerably. The Committee of Work established to standardise all regalia across the Craft reported in 1817, and by the 1820s, all English regalia followed a standard pattern based on the report's recommendations, which remains current today. Entered Apprentice aprons are plain white, the Fellowcraft's is plain

LEFT AND BELOW **Fig.13: The Sussex Plate, a drawing of the original design and a photograph from The Library and Museum of Freemasonry, London. It is never removed from its glass case as the micro-climate inside has prevented it from tarnishing.**

Image © The Library and Museum of Freemasonry, London.

white with two rosettes, while the Master Mason's apron has sky-blue edging and three rosettes. Once a Master Mason is installed as Worshipful Master the three rosettes are exchanged for inverted 'T'-shaped levels. The apron is, perhaps, the most instantly recognisable symbol of a Freemason and is a direct visual reference to the aprons worn by the medieval stonemasons. While early Freemasons' aprons tended to be quite simple if rather large, during the latter part of the eighteenth century aprons became both smaller and increasingly complex. Members of the Antient Grand Lodge in particular tended to decorate their aprons with symbols of the higher degrees, which were a popular feature of Antient working, whereas the Premier Grand Lodge (the Moderns) favoured slightly simpler designs, which referred only to the Craft degrees. However, there was little consistency between any of the aprons, which reflected personal taste as much as ritual significance.

The Library and Museum of Freemasonry in London has an extensive collection of aprons, which all show a variety of symbolism. The Moderns apron depicted (**Fig.14**) dates from just before the Union. Even though it has blue and red edging, which was generally a feature favoured by the Antients, it has quite a simple printed design which features only the three Cardinal Virtues of Faith, Hope and Charity and a few other Craft symbols: the Rising Sun in particular marks this out as a Moderns apron. The Volume of the Sacred Law and the Square and Compasses are prominently displayed in the centre of the apron and the whole design is rather simple, although it should be noted that the rosettes on the flap are positioned in quite an unusual, asymmetrical pattern. The contemporary Antients apron (**Fig.15**) is a far more complex design and features the arms of the Antient Grand Lodge, which are shown in the middle of the apron. They consist of a man, a lion, an ox and an eagle, which also feature in the design and layout of Royal Arch chapter rooms today. The flap has been overprinted with the same design as that printed underneath.

More important than issues of regalia and possibly the most contentious issue facing the newly created United Grand Lodge was the question of the 'higher degrees'. This was a very sensitive matter, especially in respect of the Royal Arch degree which was widely practised by the Antients, who considered it a fourth degree and an essential part of pure 'antient' Freemasonry, but which was ignored or even viewed with hostility by the Moderns in the Premier Grand Lodge. In the end, a compromise was reached whereby the Book of Constitutions of United Grand Lodge 'declared and pronounced that pure Antient Masonry consists of three degrees and no more, *viz.*, those of the Entered Apprentice, the Fellowcraft, and the Master Mason, including the Supreme Order of the Holy Royal Arch', which meant that the Royal Arch was effectively treated as a completion of the

ABOVE **Fig.14: Moderns Apron, c.1800-1813 in lambskin and silk.**

Image © Painton Cowan and The Library and Museum of Freemasonry, London.

Master Mason's degree. This compromise remained in force until very recently when, in 2003, the Royal Arch degree was finally recognised as being a completely separate order, although an essential culmination of the three Craft degrees. All other 'higher degrees' were left outside the jurisdiction of United Grand Lodge, in many cases setting up their

ABOVE **Fig.15: Antients Apron in white kid leather with silk backing, bearing the arms of the Antients Grand Lodge, c.1790.** *Photo © The Library and Museum of Freemasonry, London.*

own supreme bodies: Grand Mark Lodge was created in 1856 and the Supreme Council of the Ancient and Accepted Rite in 1845.

Another extremely important issue to resolve was that of ritual. The Lodge of Reconciliation reported to the new United Grand Lodge in June 1816 and the common ritual was then adopted. Over the next few years, various Lodges of Improvement were created to preserve the ritual as approved by Grand Lodge. As there has never been an authorised printed version of the ritual, the various 'workings' tend to have minor differences, even today. The Lodges of Improvement all operate under the sponsorship of a Craft lodge: one of the most common versions of ritual currently in use is known as 'Emulation' working. The Emulation Lodge of Improvement operates under the auspices of the Lodge of Unions No.256. Apart from a few minor alterations, the standard ritual has since remained unchanged.

In 1845, the Emulation Lodge of Improvement ran a competition to improve the design of the tracing boards. The winner of the competition was John Harris (c.1791-1873) who had been initiated into Freemasonry in 1818 and was, like his father, a very well-known creator of facsimiles. Harris had already been producing tracing boards since the 1820s but is most celebrated for his winning 1845 designs, which are still used today by the Emulation Lodge of Improvement and appear in every copy of the books of Emulation ritual and the *Lectures*. Harris subsequently produced tracing boards for the Royal Arch degree although these never really became popular and surviving examples are somewhat rare.

Harris' designs and execution show higher levels of technical proficiency than the earlier tracing boards produced by artists such as Bowring, although to twenty-first century eyes they may appear to be somewhat cluttered examples of Victorian eclecticism. His *Second Degree Tracing Board* (**Fig.16**) mixes various styles of architecture, including Moorish, Assyrian and Egyptian. The walls of the temple are heavily ornamented and the overall effect is of a lack of clarity: the symbolic elements become rather lost in the background. Of the three boards produced for the Emulation Lodge of Improvement in 1845, this is probably the least successful.

Perhaps due to the popularity and widespread adoption of Emulation ritual, the Harris tracing boards were for many years the most widely known and used patterns and it is possible to find many examples, which are clearly based on Harris's designs. However, new tracing board designs continued to be made, as they still are now, and when the new Freemasons' Hall was built in the 1920s in a striking Art Deco style it was felt appropriate that the tracing boards made for use in each of the lodge rooms should reflect the prevailing design of the building (**Fig.17**). These Art Deco boards, which are now nearly a hundred years old, are still in use today. They represent a move away from the naturalistic designs of Harris and are perhaps once again more like diagrams, although their sophisticated composition is both balanced and elegant. These boards are not simply lists of objects to be discussed but are designed to allow clear explanation in an aesthetically satisfying manner. Similar design values may be found in

LEFT **Fig.16: John Harris, Second Degree Tracing Board, 1845.** *Photo © Ian Allan Publishing Ltd.*

RIGHT AND FOLLOWING PAGES **Fig.17: Art Decostyle tracing boards currently in use at Freemasons' Hall, London.** *Image © The Library and Museum of Freemasonry, London.*

other near-contemporary diagrams such as Harry Beck's 1931 Tube Map for the London Underground, which is so familiar to Londoners and tourists today.

Following the Union in 1813, and since the adoption of a standard ritual in 1816, Freemasonry in England has remained ritually and organisationally stable. The political situation of Freemasonry has however, been less secure. Freemasons were persecuted by the totalitarian regimes of the twentieth century both Communist and Fascist and, perhaps understandably, Freemasonry consequently became more reclusive in its relations with the non-Masonic world. Increasingly Craft Freemasonry in England was seen as secretive and indeed sinister. Antagonism to Freemasonry culminated in the then Grand Secretary of the United Grand Lodge, Commander Michael Higham, appearing before the House of Commons Home Affairs Committee in February 1998 where he was pressed to hand over the names of members of United Grand Lodge. It is in response to such antagonism and in recognition of the fact that the Craft has been far too reclusive and inward-looking in recent years, that English Freemasonry has opened its doors to the wider world, seeking to demonstrate that its aims are, and always have been, Brotherly Love, Relief and Truth, to share its rich heritage of symbolic imagery and allegory, and to prove once again that Freemasonry can have a positive impact both at a personal level and for society in general.

E
N
S
W

E
G
N
S
W

W
S
N
E

TWO

Ascending the Winding Staircase – the Degrees of the Entered Apprentice and the Fellowcraft

Worshipful Master: *What is Freemasonry?*
Candidate: *A peculiar system of morality, veiled in allegory and illustrated by symbols.*

Before an Entered Apprentice Freemason can be 'passed' to the second or Fellowcraft's degree, he is required to answer certain questions 'in open lodge' (that is before the Master and members of the lodge which has been assembled and ceremonially 'opened') including the question listed above. Once he has answered all the questions to the satisfaction of the Worshipful Master the ceremony can proceed; hence one of the very first things an Entered Apprentice Freemason must learn about his journey through the three degrees of the Craft Freemasonry is its allegorical and symbolic nature.

Since the Union of the two Grand Lodges in 1813 and the work of the Lodge of Reconciliation which reported back to the new United Grand Lodge in 1816, Masonic ritual in England has remained more or less stable with only very minor alterations, whereas the previous one hundred and fifty years, before the Union, had seen enormous changes in both ritual practice and the use of symbolism within the Craft. It should also be noted that one of the other major effects of the Union, largely influenced by the new Grand Master the Duke of Sussex, was that English Craft and Royal Arch Freemasonry were largely de-Christianised. Although certain elements of Christian symbolism still remain in English Craft Freemasonry, other aspects have been changed to accommodate a wider religious base. Nevertheless, whilst much of the imagery of Freemasonry, especially in the narrative of the ritual dramas of the degree ceremonies themselves, derives from mainstream Judeo-Christian traditions and from the practices of operative stonemasons, this is not at all the case for all Masonic imagery. It should always be remembered, as the Masonic writer Colin Dyer put it, that 'Masonry does not live in a vacuum': it is very much affected by contemporary influences.

Many of the symbols used by the Craft and the Royal Arch are not uniquely Masonic but instead are part of a wider European cultural tradition where such symbolism was very common. For example, Dutch and Flemish still-life paintings from the sixteenth and seventeenth centuries, known as Vanitas paintings, included symbols such as skulls, candles and sandglasses, all of which were commonly understood emblems of mortality and the short nature of man's earthly existence. Such objects also featured in Masonic practice where candidates were left alone in small rooms called 'chambers of reflection', which were full of symbols of mortality, where they were left to write down their reasons for wishing to join the Fraternity and to think about the mysterious journey upon which they were about to embark. Chambers of reflection are still used in some European constitutions, and it appears that their use may be undergoing a revival in the United States; however, they are no longer found in English Craft or Royal Arch Freemasonry.

There are undoubtedly large elements of Masonic practice which refer to, amongst others, the Ancient Mystery religions of Greece and Egypt, the Jewish cabbala, the Hermetic Tradition, classical architecture, Neo-Platonism and the Rosicrucian Order, however it would be quite wrong to suggest, as others have, that Freemasonry has an unbroken link with any of these traditions. It is possible that some of these elements may have originated from the journeys made by European travellers, including Freemasons, to the Middle East in the late eighteenth and early nineteenth centuries. The ancient ruins of Mithraic temples, for example, may well have suggested parallels with Masonic working: symbols such as ladders appear in both Freemasonry and Mithraic practice, which also included rites of progression. Some attempts to connect Masonic symbolism directly to the Ancient Mysteries, although undoubtedly sincere, are probably the result of wishful thinking instead of sound scholarship. For example, the Library and Museum of Freemasonry has in its collection an early twentieth century drawing of a purported 'Egyptian Rite', which attempted, perhaps somewhat tenuously, to link ancient Egyptian imagery to Masonic practice.

Rather than descending directly from the Ancient Mystery religions it seems far more likely that such elements were brought into speculative Freemasonry by its non-operative members who found a natural framework for their mystical interests in the practices of operative stonemasons in their lodges, not least because of the importance of Geometry. Active stonemasons placed great significance on the science of Geometry because it was essential to both architecture and construction, while the speculative Freemasons were highly appreciative of its influence on Neo-Platonic thinking.

Very early speculative Freemasonry does appear to have attracted men with mystical interests: Elias Ashmole published a catalogue of British alchemical works, *Theatrum Chemicum Britannicum*, in 1652 and his contemporary, the Scottish Freemason Sir Robert Moray (c.1609-1673), was a patron of the alchemist Thomas Vaughan (1621-1666). Both Ashmole and Moray were Fellows of the Royal Society, as were many later Freemasons. Some Masonic historians have calculated that in the early years of the eighteenth century between a third and half the Fellows of the Royal Society were Freemasons, implying a strong link between intellectual endeavour and Freemasonry. The Premier Grand Lodge even followed Royal Society practice by forbidding the discussion of religion or politics at lodge meetings, a prohibition which remains in force today.

Quite how it came to be that such non-operative stonemasons became members of operative stonemasons' lodges is unclear. It may simply have been that men like Ashmole sought the company of senior operative stonemasons who were themselves educated men, well-versed in the Seven Liberal Arts and Sciences, especially Geometry, which featured so strongly in the educational framework of the time. We know that Ashmole was initiated into a lodge in Warrington in 1646 but there is also a record of his being admitted into a fellowship known as the Acception in 1682. The Acception appears to have been an inner circle of one of the London Livery Companies, the London Company of Masons, and seems to have been active in the late seventeenth century, although it may just have been a spiritual forerunner of speculative Freemasonry, which developed so rapidly in the 1720s.

Early Masonic ritual generally took the form of a catechism, with more esoteric ritual normally restricted to the admission of candidates. More modern working, especially after the Union of the two Grand Lodges in 1813, has tended to concentrate on ritual to a greater extent: the catechisms still exist as *The Lectures of the Three Degrees of Craft Masonry* and are occasionally 'worked' by lodges, although this seems to be quite rare. The *Lectures* contain a great deal of explanation of both the ritual working and the symbols found in each degree, most of which are illustrated on the tracing board of the degree. The second and third degree tracing boards are explained, at least in part, during their respective ceremonies, whereas the first degree tracing board, like the *Lectures*, is rarely presented in open lodge. Arthur Thistleton's *First Degree Tracing Board* of 1836 is an interesting mid-nineteenth-century example.

Arthur Thistleton (1794-1842) was a lesser-known artist working in London in the 1830s, whose tracing boards are quite similar to the early designs of John Harris, whose 1845 boards appear in every book of Emulation ritual. Thistleton painted a set of boards for the Ivanhoe Lodge in Ashby-de-la-Zouche (constituted 1836, erased 1851) in 1836 and a very similar set at about the same time for the Lodge of Regularity No.91 in London. His *First Degree Tracing Board* (**Fig. 18**) contains nearly all the elements found in post-Union tracing boards, and it is interesting to note that he intended this board to have artistic as well a symbolic value. For example, he took care to 'marble' the black and white pavement to represent marble floor-tiles. Although there is no real attempt to place the objects on the board in a convincing three-dimensional space and few of the objects really relate to each

ABOVE **Fig.18: Arthur Thistleton, First Degree Tracing Board painted for Ivanhoe Lodge, Ashby-de-la-Zouche, 1836.** *Photo © Terence Haunch.*

other spatially, this tracing board is a great deal more than a simple diagram: the ritual objects have been positioned not only to reflect their symbolic significance but also to produce an elegantly constructed composition. The objects themselves have been painted with care and some precision: the grain of the wood of the Square, Level and Plumb Rule is clearly visible and the columns are quite deftly painted, even if their classical proportions are incorrect.

In terms of its symbolic content, the tracing board is surrounded by a tessellated border with the compass-points inset and it has tassels at its corners. Interestingly, Thistleton's second and third degree tracing boards also have the compass-points marked, which is somewhat unusual as they are usually found only on first degree tracing boards. In the central part of the tracing board there are three columns, their capitals belonging to three different classical orders of architecture. The columns rest on a chequered pavement, and visible between them are two blocks of stone, one unshaped and the other apparently finished: the Rough and Perfect Ashlars. On the Rough Ashlar rests the Chisel, a tool which helps transform the rough-hewn stone into a polished building block. Above the Ashlars are a board with a plan on it (a 'true' tracing board, used by operative stonemasons when drawing up their plans) and to the other side a Plumb Rule, a symbol of uprightness. Above the columns are the Twenty-Four Inch Gauge for the twenty-four hours of the day, the Heavy Maul, also used in shaping the Ashlars, the Blazing Star, a symbol of the Supreme Being, and the lifting-device known as a Lewis. A Lewis is a set of wedge-shaped metal plates which can be inserted into a suitable cavity on the top of a block of stone: under tension they enable the block to be lifted into place by a hoist or derrick.

In the top half of the tracing board are a mason's Square symbolising morality, a Level representing equality, and a diagram of a circle with a point in the centre, flanked by two parallel lines. Finally, there is an open Bible, with a set of Compasses and a Square resting on it, supporting a ladder with three blocked steps; to one side is the Sun, and to the other the Moon surrounded by seven stars.

During the ceremony of initiation the candidate is brought into the lodge room blindfolded. He is then asked a series of questions to ensure that he is voluntarily seeking to become a Freemason and to confirm his reasons for wanting to join the Craft. The aspiring Freemason will then undertake an obligation to keep confidential the 'secrets and mysteries of the order'. After the initiate has undertaken his obligation his blindfold is removed and the Worshipful Master then explains the symbolism of some of the ritual objects found in the lodge room. Although the first degree tracing board is visible, it is not usually drawn to the attention of the initiate and is now rarely explained in full, even though it contains much of the symbolism of both the lodge room itself and the Ceremony of Initiation.

The first objects pointed out to the initiate by the Worshipful Master are described as the Three Greater Lights: the Volume of the Sacred Law, the Square and the Compasses, all of which are on the Worshipful Master's pedestal and are depicted towards the top of the tracing board. The Volume of the Sacred Law refers to whichever text the initiate himself holds as being sacred. Whilst the Volume of the Sacred Law normally displayed in the lodge room will reflect the faith of the majority of the lodge's members, it is important that each candidate takes all of his obligations on the book that he considers most sacred. In England, most lodges will display the Bible, while Jewish candidates will take their obligations on the Tanakh, Muslim candidates will use the Koran and Hindus either the Rig Veda or the Bhagavad Gita. It is not unheard of today for Deist candidates to take their obligations on a copy of the Laws of Physics: what matters is a professed belief in some form of Supreme Being, for under the jurisdiction of the United Grand Lodge of England an atheist may not be made a Freemason. It is indicative of the innate religious tolerance of modern Freemasonry that lodges in Israel, a country with many sectarian divisions, give equal precedence to the Tanakh, Bible and Koran at their meetings. Indeed the Great Seal of the Grand Lodge of Israel contains not only the Square and Compasses but also the three symbols of the faiths held by the majority of its members, namely the Star of David, the Crescent and the Cross.

The sacred writings are to define and express the Freemason's faith, whatever that may be, whilst the Square and Compasses are together symbols of Freemasonry itself. Their significance is only alluded to in the first degree: their deeper meaning is not fully revealed until the third degree. This hidden meaning is itself symbolised by the fact that both the points of the Compasses lie beneath the Square rather than on top of it.

Most of the remaining symbols on the tracing board are not explained during the first degree ceremony as normally performed. Nevertheless, it is interesting to note how these symbols and objects suggest not only their own origins but the ritual sources of Freemasonry itself. Symbols derived from the traditions of operative stonemasons include the various stonemasons' tools as well as the two blocks of stone: the Ashlars. The Rough Ashlar is an unformed lump of stone straight from the quarry, and represents the newly initiated Entered Apprentice at the start of his Masonic Journey. The smoothed and finished Perfect Ashlar symbolises the fully-fledged Master Mason, educated, fully trained and ready to accept his responsibilities as a member of society.

The Twenty-Four Inch Gauge, Gavel and Chisel are the operative instruments used by stonemasons to transform the rough-hewn block into a usable building stone (**Fig. 19**). The Gauge represents the twenty-four hours of the day and how those hours should be spent, whilst the Gavel symbolises conscience, and the Chisel education. At a deeper level the Gavel might be seen as a symbol of energy and passion, whereas the Chisel, by directing that energy, may be interpreted as a means of analysis and classification, and hence an intellectual counterweight to passion. The Gauge, as an instrument of measurement, enables the tools to work together, both literally and metaphorically, thereby establishing balance between energy and analysis.

Symbols from Biblical sources include the ladder which, according to the *Lectures*, is Jacob's Ladder from the Old Testament and represents the Freemason's path to Heaven. The three blocked steps in Thistleton's *First Degree Tracing Board* are more normally represented by a cross, an anchor and a heart, or sometimes by three female figures, one with a small child, representing the Christian Theological Virtues of Faith, Hope and Charity. The four tassels at the corners of the tracing board represent the Four Cardinal Virtues of Temperance, Fortitude, Justice and Mercy. These four virtues are more explicitly depicted on the mosaic ceiling of Grand Temple in Freemasons' Hall in London.

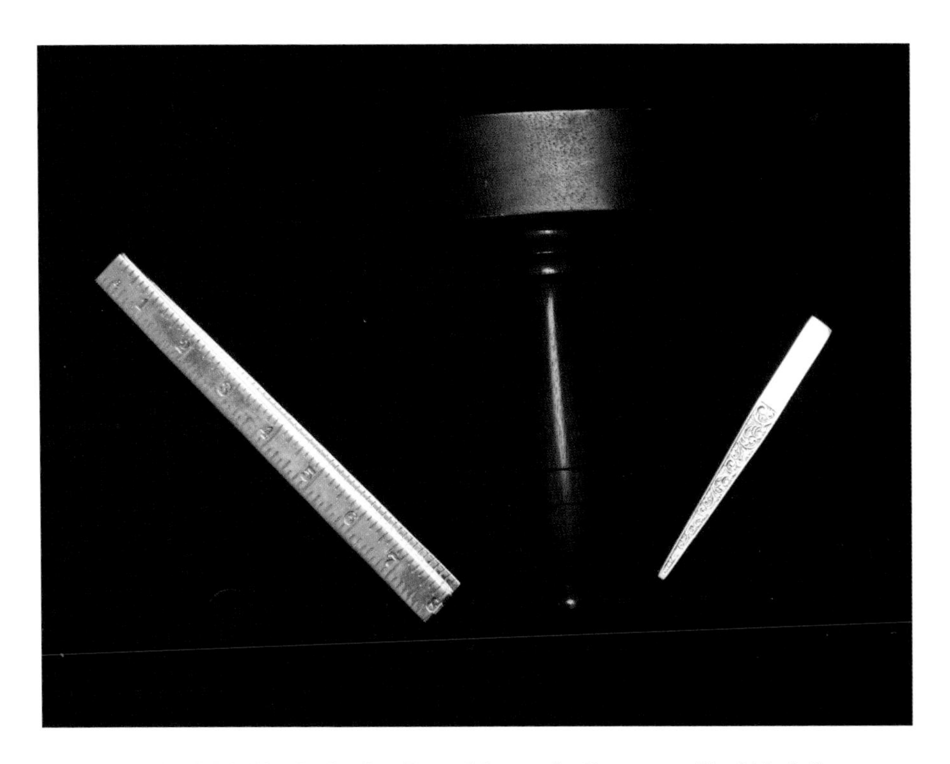

ABOVE **Fig.19: Working Tools of an Entered Apprentice Freemason. The 24 Inch Gauge, Gavel and Chisel.** *Image © Philip Bennison.*

The black and white Mosaic Pavement is a reference to the floor of King Solomon's Temple, again from the Bible, but it also has a more mystical meaning as it symbolises the opposing natures of our existence: joy and sorrow, night and day, good and evil. It is interesting to note how some tracing board designers, like Thistleton, have used the orthogonals of the Mosaic Pavement to create a fictive three-dimensional setting for the columns, although perhaps rarely as successfully as Josiah Bowring in his *First Degree Tracing Board* of 1819. Even so, the fictive space both Bowring and Thistleton create is not intended to be at all naturalistic: it remains a ritual space.

The three columns depict three of the Five Noble Orders of Architecture: the Doric, Ionic and Corinthian, which were the originally established by the Greeks. The Romans adopted these three Greek Orders of Architecture in the first century BC and adapted two

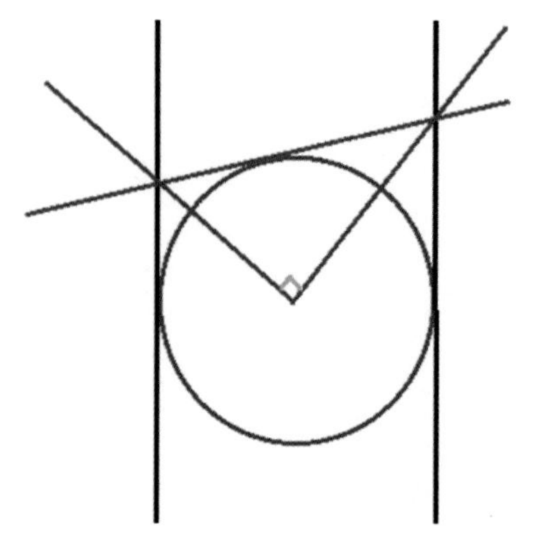

LEFT **Fig.20: Derivation of a right angle from a circle flanked by two parallel lines.** *Image © Huw Pritchard*

of them to make two further Orders: the Tuscan was a simpler, even more austere form of the Doric and the Composite an elaborate mixture of Ionic and Corinthian elements. Each of the orders represents an important figure from Masonic legend and is therefore his symbol. Solomon, King of Israel, who embodies Wisdom, is represented by the Ionic Order; Hiram King of Tyre by the Doric Order and hence Strength; finally there is the important Masonic figure of Hiram Abiff, the legendary architect of King Solomon's Temple, who is personified by the Corinthian Order, signifying Beauty. In the early ritual working of the Moderns of the Premier Grand Lodge the Ionic and Corinthian Orders were reversed, as was the case in Cole's tracing board designs.

Each order stipulated a different height-to-diameter ratio for the columns (although the actual ratios used in practice tended to vary considerably), hence a Doric column should have a height equal to seven diameters, an Ionic column eight diameters and a Corinthian column nine diameters. Thistleton's columns are clearly arranged in a row because of their position on the Mosaic Pavement and yet are all of the same height, implying that either he was not aware of the necessary height-to-diameter ratios or was ignoring the convention. Bowring, on the other hand, places his columns at different depths within his picture frame, thereby allowing perspective to take care of the height difference without interfering with his compositional scheme.

The concept underpinning the Noble Orders of Architecture is that perfection in both art and architecture can be defined by rules: this is a Vitruvian concept and therefore not at all innovative. Thomas Chippendale (1718-1779), however, considered it so important that he included a discussion of the Five Noble Orders of Architecture in the preface to the 1754 edition of his *Gentleman and Cabinet Maker's Director*.

Possibly the most abstract symbol appearing on the first degree tracing board is that of the point within a circle flanked by two parallel lines (**Fig. 20**). In some ways, this one symbol encapsulates much of the symbolism of Freemasonry. In pre-Union ritual, the two parallel lines were said to represent St. John the Baptist and St. John the Evangelist, who were both patron saints of stonemasons. After the Union the two 'Grand Parallels' became Moses and King Solomon. The point within a circle itself can be interpreted as a Freemason in the centre bounded by his duty or as a symbol of the Supreme Being surrounded by the orbit of the Sun. This is not to suggest that any of the meanings are mutually exclusive: on the contrary, Masonic symbolism can hold many layers of meaning. For example, the point within a circle can also be understood in operative terms as a geometric method of deriving a right angle. By drawing two radians from the centre of the circle and extending them to the flanking parallel lines and then joining these intersections with a line which is tangential to the circle the resultant angle at the centre will be a right angle of 90°.

ABOVE **Fig.21: Josiah Bowring, Second Degree Tracing Board of the Lodge of Honor and Generosity No.165, 1819.** *Image © The Library and Museum of Freemasonry, London.*

The symbolism of the second degree is perhaps less extensive than the first degree and concentrates mainly on the building of King Solomon's Temple. It may not have the same mystical dimension that is so central to both the third degree in Craft Freemasonry and the degree of the Holy Royal Arch, but it does introduce one of the most satisfying and meaningful allegories of Freemasonry: the Winding Staircase.

Arguably, the most striking elements of Josiah Bowring's 1819 *Second Degree Tracing Board* (**Fig. 21**) are the two golden columns flanking a neoclassical temple with a chamber, accessed by a curved staircase. The ritual itself spends a considerable time discussing the nature and importance of the columns and states that they are named *Jachin* and *Boaz*, which names were used as the title of a famous Masonic exposé of 1762. The ritual also explains the

LEFT **Fig.22: Second degree Tracing Board of the Lodge in the 7th Light Dragoons, English, c.1810.** *Image © The Library and Museum of Freemasonry, London.*

subject-matter of the lower picture which illustrates an Old Testament account of an incident following Jephthah's battle against the Ephraimites: rather gruesomely in the background of the lower panel the tiny figure of a Gileadite soldier can be seen beheading an Ephraimite insurgent.

Not all second degree tracing boards are quite as explicit in their depiction of the aftermath of Jephthah's battle. The lower section of the *Second Degree Tracing Board of the Lodge in the 7th Light Dragoons* of c.1810 (**Fig. 22**) still shows the bridge over the river Jordan which the Ephraimites attempted to use on their escape from the army of Jephthah. On the riverfront may be seen some of the bodies of the slaughtered Ephraimite fugitives, although their execution is not shown as it is on Bowring's board. Interestingly, on close inspection, the tents of the Ephraimite encampment appear to be the ridge tents typically used by the early nineteenth century military, which would be entirely appropriate for a military lodge operating at that time.

The Lodge in the 7th Light Dragons was established in 1807 under the re-issued Antients Warrant No.262 and subsequently re-numbered following the Union in 1813 as No.331, when it was in the 7th Hussars. Upon its closure in 1824, the lodge sent its box of Masonic equipment to the Grand Secretary to be sold for the benefit of the Orphan Fund. The lodge was a travelling lodge in that it met wherever the Regiment was stationed; all its furniture (including the tracing boards, which were kept on rollers) was kept in quite a

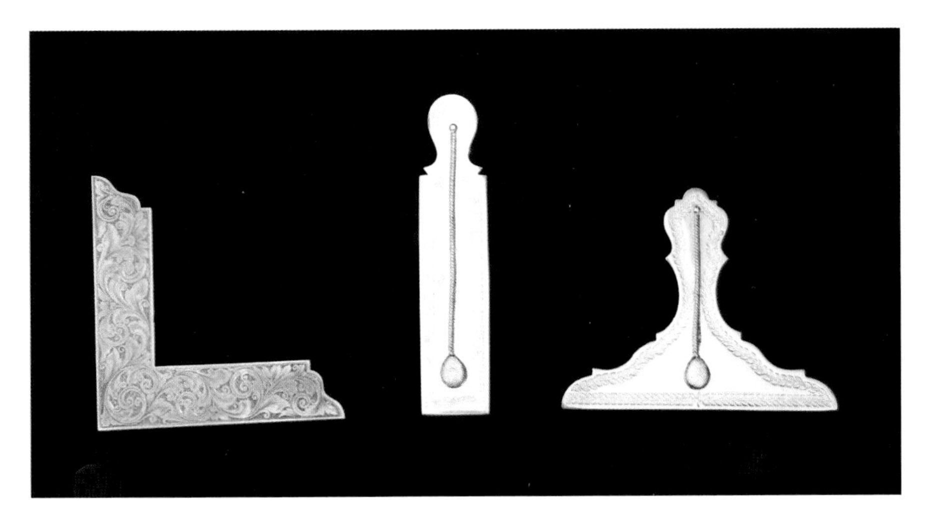

ABOVE **Fig.23: Working Tools of a Fellowcraft Freemason. The Square, Level and Plumb Rule.**

Image © Philip Bennison.

small box of approximately 60 cm square. As the 7th Dragoons served in the Peninsular War (1808-1814) and the 7th Hussars fought with some distinction at the Battle of Waterloo (18 June 1815), it is certainly possible that the box would have been in the baggage-train near the battlefield.

The overall effect of this attractive Tracing Board is of a well-constructed, no-nonsense image, entirely in keeping with its first owners. The Temple in the top section has been depicted in an accurately rendered Regency Gothick style: the three statues on the top of the Temple represent the three original Grand Masters, with one placed, perhaps somewhat improbably, directly onto the central dome. However, the perspective of the Mosaic Pavement at the bottom of the Winding Staircase appears to be inconsistent with that at the top. The network at the top of the two pillars is also somewhat unusual as it covers almost all of the capitals. The painting of the two wardens at the foot and top of the Winding Staircase is quite painterly in execution; although the brush strokes are very fine they are clearly visible.

In terms of the Freemason's journey, the most important elements concern the operative stonemason's tools, the Winding Staircase and the room at the top of the staircase. The Fellowcraft's tools (**Fig. 23**) are the Square, Level and Plumb Rule, and their meanings, according to the *Lectures*, correspond to Morality, Equality and Uprightness respectively. Unlike the Entered Apprentice's tools, the Fellowcraft's are exclusively tools of measurement: the Masonic writer W. Kirk MacNulty argues that the Level symbolises 'restraint' and the Plumb Rule 'licence', while the Square, as Morality, defines the judgement to be applied in their use.

The *Lectures* and the second degree ritual both explain that the Winding Staircase consisted of three, five or seven steps, matching the number of ritual 'steps' taken by candidates during the three degree ceremonies. The first three steps of the staircase refer to the first three Grand Masters: Solomon King of Israel, Hiram King of Tyre and Hiram Abiff. The five steps of the staircase symbolise the Five Noble Orders of Architecture (the three Greek orders of the Doric, Ionic and Corinthian and the additional two Roman orders of the Tuscan and Composite) while the last seven steps represent the Seven Liberal Arts and Sciences: Grammar, Rhetoric, Logic, Arithmetic, Geometry, Music and Astronomy.

The Winding Staircase also has a deeper significance, in that it represents the Freemason's own journey and is therefore a metaphor for Freemasonry itself. At the bottom of the Winding Staircase stands the Junior Warden, who will prevent any unqualified Freemason from ascending it, whilst at the top is positioned the Senior Warden who will only allow fully-qualified Fellowcraft Freemasons to enter the room glimpsed behind him. This room is the Middle Chamber of King Solomon's Temple and it was here that the Fellowcraft stonemasons building King Solomon's Temple received their wages: Entered Apprentices simply received board and lodging, whilst the more highly qualified Fellowcrafts were paid in coin. Such advancement had to be earned through hard work and self-improvement. In operative terms, a stonemason would have to serve out his apprenticeship to earn the pay of a journeyman, whereas the speculative Freemason would need to become educated in the Seven Liberal Arts and Sciences before advancing further in Freemasonry.

In 1687 Sir Isaac Newton (1643-1727) published his *Philosophiae Naturalis Principia Mathematica* in which he described the Laws of Motion, thereby showing that Nature followed certain laws which could not only be understood by man using reason and empirical methodology but which enabled accurate predictions to be made. Its publication even prompted the poet Alexander Pope (1688-1744) to write 'Nature and Nature's Laws lay hid in night: God said '*Let Newton be!*' and all was light.' Although there seems to be no evidence that Newton was himself a Freemason it is known that Desaguliers, the third Grand Master of the Premier Grand Lodge and subsequently Deputy Grand Master to later aristocratic Grand Masters, was possibly the foremost proponent of Newtonian thinking at the time and gave many public lectures on Natural Philosophy. It is an indication of the intellectual nature of some lodges that there is significant evidence that similar lectures were often presented at lodge meetings. As an example, the minutes of a music club for Freemasons, the short-lived *Philo-Musicae et Architecturae Societas Apollini* (which only existed between 1725 and 1727), contain a dissertation on the Seven Liberal Arts and Sciences including an exploration of the relationship between music and mathematics: it describes music and geometry as 'twin sisters'. The importance of geometry to Masonic philosophy cannot be overstated: geometry was not only the means by which Man could understand the world, and therefore his place in it, but also ultimately a means to acquire knowledge of himself. As an early twentieth-century Masonic historian, Walter L Wilmshurst (1867-1939), wrote: 'Geometry, therefore, is synonymous with self-knowledge'.

The ritual explanation of the second degree tracing board notes that the Middle Chamber has within it 'certain Hebrew characters' which are often represented by the letter 'G', which stands for 'God, the Grand Geometrician of the Universe'. Bowring's *Second Degree Tracing Board* uses a Hebrew letter to represent the letter 'G', whilst other boards are more explicit: the letter 'G' is more clearly visible above the entrance to the chamber in *The Second Degree Tracing Board of the Lodge in the 7th Light Dragoons*, for example. Colin Dyer notes that Prichard's *Masonry Dissected* of 1730 gives its meaning as simply 'Geometry', and it should also be noted that French tracing boards of the period also use the letter 'G' rather than 'D' for 'Dieu' as might be expected had it simply meant God. In fact, Geometry would appear to be something more than simply a Neo-Platonic reference to the Supreme Being. Not only was it one of the Seven Liberal Arts and Sciences and at the heart of both architecture and hence operative stonemasonry, it was also entirely consistent with medieval images of God as designer of all Creation who is often depicted in illustrated manuscripts and even stained-glass windows holding a pair of Compasses.

In spite of the rationalist nature of much Enlightenment thinking, the eighteenth century remained profoundly religious. Newton's Laws might have described the world, but to the eighteenth-century mind its apparently designed nature implied a designer. In speculative Freemasonry God as Grand Geometrician of the Universe is a central feature of the Middle Chamber: the chamber itself can be seen as a symbol of the human soul, which needs to absorb the moral lessons of the first and second degrees in preparation for the more mystical teachings of the third degree and ultimately the Royal Arch.

THREE

The Mystical Journey of the Master Mason to the Holy Royal Arch

For the medieval stonemason, the Master Mason was the highly important figure in charge of all building work on site: only the Master Mason had the right to employ other masons and it was the Master Mason who decided how the construction should be built. However, in speculative terms the Master Mason's Degree represents the final step of Craft Freemasonry, but this does not mean that the Master Mason has been Master of his lodge. On the contrary, it is normally only after a Freemason has been raised to the third degree of a Master Mason that he may start his progression towards the Master's chair.

It appears that very early speculative Freemasonry consisted of two degrees: the Entered Apprentice and the Fellowcraft; indeed Fellowcrafts held the office of Worshipful Master of their lodges. However, by the time of the formation of the Antient Grand Lodge in 1751, it is clear that a separate Master Mason's degree had been in existence for at least twenty years. Although it was not at first a normal part of Masonic progression, in fact it was often necessary to join a different Master's Lodge in order to receive the degree.

For most Master Masons, the mystical nature of the third degree ceremony is such that it is a far more memorable occasion than their initiation; Wilmshurst described it as 'the real initiation'. The candidate enters a darkened room lit by one candle on the Worshipful Master's pedestal; on the floor is the representation of an open grave. The ceremony recreates the legendary story of the murder of Hiram Abiff, the chief architect of King Solomon's Temple who was killed by three Fellowcrafts who had first tried to force him to reveal the secrets of a Master Mason. The moment of his death is re-enacted and the candidate is laid on the floor onto an image of a grave, much as was done in the middle of the eighteenth century (**Fig.24**).

The ceremony continues with the discovery of the body of Hiram Abiff by a group of trustworthy Fellowcrafts who had been sent to look for him and had found his body in a shallow grave. Before reporting back to King Solomon, they marked the position of the grave with a sprig of acacia.

On returning to recover the body of Hiram Abiff the recovering party were at first unable to raise his body out of the grave, and it was only when one of the party took a particularly firm grip of the body that they were able to do so. This moment is recreated by the Worshipful Master who, with the assistance of the Senior and Junior Wardens, raises the candidate back to a standing position. This very dramatic and deeply mystical part of the ceremony not only invites the new Master Mason to consider the inevitable prospect of death but also points to the spiritual re-awakening of a Freemason.

ABOVE **Fig.24: Eighteenth century print of the third degree ceremony. Assembly of Freemasons for the Reception of members to the Degree of Master-Mason. Plate V from J.M. Bernigeroth, Les Coutumes des Francs-Maçons dans leurs Assemblées (1745).**

Image © The Library and Museum of Freemasonry, London.

Although there is an obvious superficial resemblance with the Christian doctrine of the Resurrection it should be stressed here that, whilst it does require a belief in a Supreme Being, Freemasonry is not a religion and there is in no sense any form of 'Masonic after-life' or any other religious dogma. The spiritual re-birth experienced by the new Master Mason is entirely of the nature of a spiritual renewal within his own personal belief system: a new way of life.

The next part of the ceremony is conducted with normal lighting restored and continues the explanation of the Hiramic legend, including an explanation of the third degree tracing board, all examples of which portray a coffin with emblems of mortality. Although on some (mainly pre-Union) examples, such as Josiah Bowring's *Third Degree Tracing Board of the Lodge of Harmony No.255* (**Fig. 25**), the coffin is opened to display the body of Hiram Abiff with his injuries visible. The ritual completes the Hiramic legend by

ABOVE **Fig.25: Third Degree Tracing Board of the Lodge of Harmony No.255, possibly by Josiah Bowring, probably before 1813.** *Photo © Terence Haunch.*

ABOVE **Fig.26: John Harris, Third Degree Tracing Board, 1845.** *Photo © Ian Allan Publishing Ltd.*

explaining how the three murderous Fellowcrafts were found hiding in a cave, as shown at the bottom of Bowring's board, and then describes how Hiram was buried with full honours as near to the Sanctum Sanctorum, or the Holy of Holies, as Israelite law permitted. The third degree tracing board nearly always depicts the three murder weapons used: the Plumb Rule, Level and the Heavy Maul, which struck the final blow.

The *Third Degree Tracing Board of the Lodge of Harmony No.255*, probably painted by Josiah Bowring, is a fairly typical example of the 'open-coffin' style of early third degree tracing boards. In depicting the dead body of Hiram Abiff with a small vignette of the murderous Fellowcrafts hiding in a cave, it is possibly less effective than Harris' later tracing board in which the closed coffin and more convincingly rendered ritual space are more powerfully evocative of mortality (**Fig. 26**).

Harris' striking design may be of the closed-coffin form but it still traces its descent from earlier designs by John Cole and Josiah Bowring. The coffin is depicted in the naturalistic manner favoured in the middle of the nineteenth century, as if looking down into the grave. At the top of the coffin are the working tools of the degree, namely the Skirret, Pencil and Compasses, whilst at the foot of the coffin are the murder weapons of the Hiramic legend. The coffin itself and the Skull and Crossbones are traditional symbols of mortality, while the image on the scroll is of the Sanctum Sanctorum near to which, according to Hiramic legend, the body of the murdered Hiram Abiff was finally interred.

The lighting effect painted by Harris is much more dramatic than on the earlier Bowring-type boards. The obliquely-lit Skull and Crossbones create an eerie sense of mortality which is perhaps more effective than Bowring's open coffin: rather than simply feeling a sense of shock and horror at the fate of the stricken architect the candidate is instead struck with a stronger sense of his own mortality.

The writing on the Harris' coffin is in a simple Masonic cipher, which he had adapted. The letters of the plate of the coffin read, from right to left in the Hebrew fashion, 'HAB' (Hiram Abiff) followed by 'AL 3000' which stands for Anno Lucis 3000, the year of Hiram's murder. Anno Lucis, sometimes translated as 'in the year of Masonic light', pre-dates the current era by 4,000 years; hence Hiram's murder allegedly took place in the year 1000 BCE. Underneath the Skull and Crossbones are the letters 'MB' repeated, representing the two different versions of the words spoken by those who discovered the body of Hiram Abiff as recounted in the third degree ceremony, one as used by the Moderns and the other by the Antients.

Harris' *Third Degree Tracing Board* is possibly the most effective of the three tracing boards from 1845. It lacks the slightly pompous feel of his *First Degree Tracing Board* and the cluttered eclecticism of his *Second Degree Tracing Board* and serves both to illustrate the Hiramic legend and to act as a suitably sombre and evocative reminder of the inevitability of death.

The working tools of a Master Mason (**Fig. 27**) arguably reflect the more spiritual nature of the Master Mason Degree. One of the tools, the Skirret (an implement used to run out lines in order to mark out the outline of an intended structure), is a later post-Union introduction which appears on Harris boards from about 1825. The Skirret is joined by the Pencil and Compasses, all three being tools of design and creativity which are used in the creation of a building. The *Lectures* compare the Skirret to the Volume of the Sacred Law, as the lines it marks represent the limits we should set on our own conduct. The Pencil, meanwhile, is an implement used by our sense of creativity, which can only flourish if it is ordered and organised. The Compasses define the correct proportions, which are then outlined by the Skirret. It can be argued that the deeper symbolism of the Master Mason's working tools is that the Pencil is an image of our active thoughts which, in order to be effective, must be ordered by a framework, i.e. our ability to understand. This sense of understanding is symbolised by the Skirret. Both are then held in balance by our consciousness, represented by the Compasses.

It might seem surprising that the Compasses form part of the third degree working tools whilst their normal counterpart, the Square, forms part of the second degree working

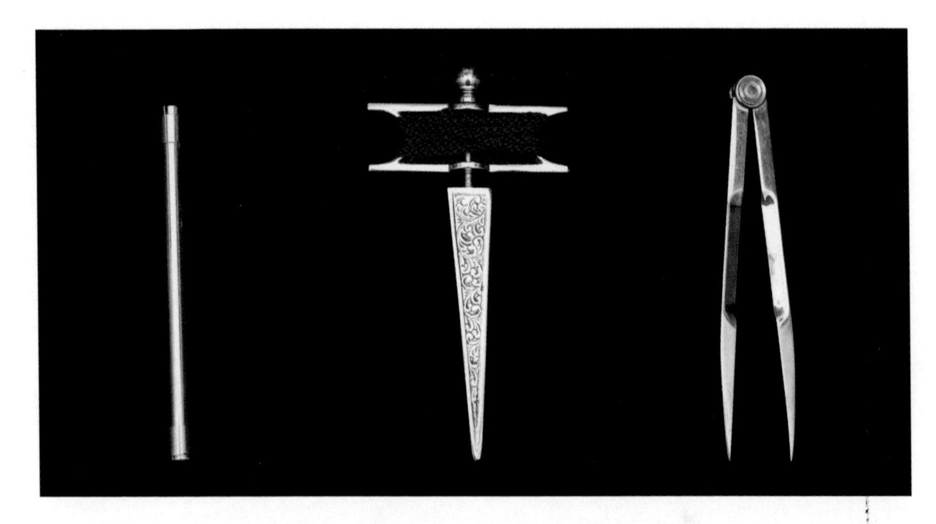

ABOVE **Fig.27: Working Tools of a Master Mason. The Pencil, Skirret and Compasses.**

Image © Philip Bennison.

tools, but it is important to see the Square and Compasses both as separate objects and as a conjoined symbol. After every obligation in Craft Freemasonry, the first objects drawn to the attention of the candidate are the Square and Compasses, seen as a pair, placed on the Volume of the Sacred Law. These three together are described as the Three Great Lights of Freemasonry. As the Freemason progresses through the three degrees of Craft Freemasonry, the points of the Compasses are progressively revealed as marks of his progress. Indeed, on being raised to the third degree the new Master Mason is told that he may use the Compasses freely 'to render the circle of [his] Masonic duties complete'. The Volume of the Sacred Law will always be whichever book the candidate himself holds as being central to his own beliefs. In English Lodges this is usually a copy of the Bible, although this is by no means always the case, whilst the Square and Compasses together, as a symbol both of spirituality and Freemasonry itself, are universal to the ritual.

It is quite common for lodge members to give a presentation-set of a Square and Compasses to their own lodges. The examples here belonged to Neptune Lodge No.22 which was founded in December 1757 (**Fig. 28**). The Square has the inscription 'The Worshipful Lodge No. XIII' on its face and a presentation inscription: 'This Square with a Pair of Silver Compasses was Presented to Lodge No. XIII by Brs. Emanuel Miller and

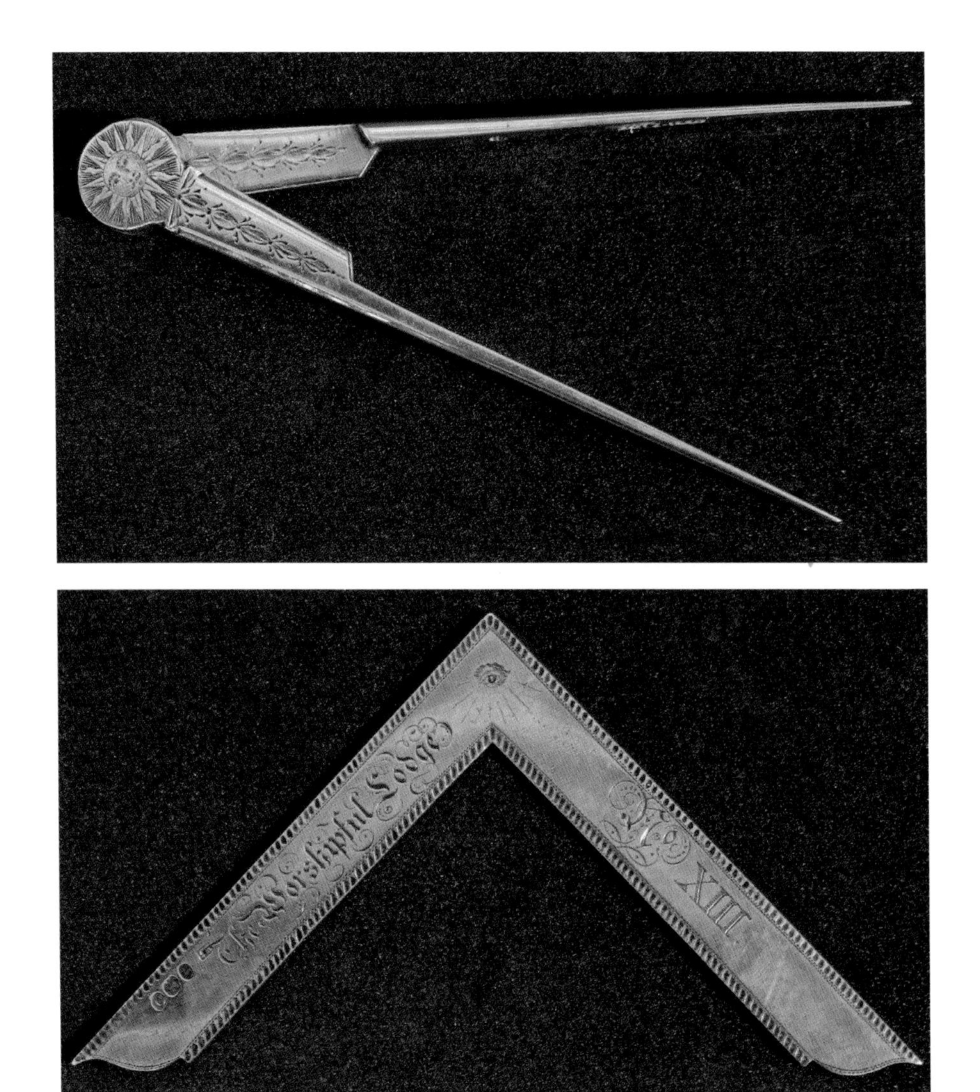

ABOVE **Fig.28: Square and Compasses of Neptune Lodge No.22, 1810.**

Image © The Library and Museum of Freemasonry, London.

ABOVE AND RIGHT **Fig.29: World War One Square and Compasses.** *Image © The Library and Museum of Freemasonry, London.*

Henry Parsons February 13th 1810' on the reverse. On its founding, under the Antient Grand Lodge, Neptune Lodge's number was 64A which it kept until the re-numbering of July 1759. It is possible that the engraved words 'Worshipful Lodge No.XIII' refer to its lodge number immediately before the Union in 1813 when it was re-numbered No.22, however this is no more than speculation.

Both the Square and Compasses of Neptune Lodge were cast in silver and have been embellished by hand-chasing to the edges and engraving. The Square has a representation of the all-seeing eye at the angle of the obverse side. The Compasses have an image of the Sun at the hinge, and foliage motifs on the arms. The style of both, whilst clearly decorative and ceremonial, is unfussy and unpretentious.

Although it is very common for lodges to have sets of highly decorated working tools, including Squares and Compasses, it is by no means essential. For example, The Library and Museum of Freemasonry has sets of much cruder Squares and Compasses used in Masonic meetings by British Freemasons on active service during the First World War (1914-1918), some of which were made by the soldiers themselves, although there are examples which were made by local farmers in exchange for food (**Fig. 29**). Such rough and ready Squares and Compasses have a poignant simplicity when compared to the more splendid set owned by Neptune Lodge No.22, and yet, and above all, it is the symbolic significance of the two together which is most important, signifying Freemasonry as a whole. When the letter G is added, they become a symbol of the Supreme Being, the G representing both 'God' and 'Geometry': God as the Grand Geometrician. The rather crude examples of Squares and Compasses used by First World War soldiers in Flanders convey the same symbolic meaning as the splendid set presented to Neptune Lodge No.22.

Although the third degree introduces ideas of spirituality into the ritual, especially when inviting the new Master Mason to consider his own mortality which he should face with courage, it also contains lessons about his conduct with other people. It stresses the importance of not betraying trust and of supporting those in need regardless of whether they are Freemasons or not. The often stated assertion that Freemasons give preferential treatment to other Freemasons is a myth: a fact which the United Grand Lodge, for obvious reasons, takes care to explain in its literature. In popular culture such preferential treatment was even satirised in an episode of *The Simpsons* when the fictitious 'Stonecutters' were able to have parking-tickets cancelled and received many similar 'perks'. More seriously, there have even been claims that criminal Freemasons have made covert Masonic signs to judges at their trials in the hope of more lenient treatment. Happily, or perhaps unhappily for the criminals concerned, such entreaties appear to have been ineffectual.

In 1911 the murderer Frederick Seddon, who was a Freemason and who was being tried for the grisly murder of a female lodger, attempted to avoid the death penalty by making Masonic signs at the presiding judge, Mr Justice Bucknil, whom he knew to be a Freemason and who promptly told him to stop. Seddon was convicted and, when asked if he had anything to say before sentencing, protested his innocence in the name of 'The Great Architect of the Universe', an explicitly Masonic term referring to the Supreme Being. Mr Justice Bucknil's reply, before sentencing him to death, was unequivocal: 'You and I both belong to the same brotherhood and it is all the more painful for me to have to say what I am saying. But our brotherhood does not encourage crime; on the contrary it condemns it. I pray you again to make your peace with the Great Architect of the Universe.' The importance of high standards of moral conduct is a recurring theme throughout Masonic ritual and is central to the Hiramic legend.

An important ritual aspect of the Hiramic lesson is that the secrets of a Master Mason were split between the three original Grand Masters, i.e. King Solomon, Hiram King of Tyre and the murdered Hiram Abiff, which meant that with Hiram Abiff's death the secrets had been lost. In order for the remaining masons to be able to function and so complete the building of the Temple, King Solomon ordered that 'substituted secrets' be put in place and it is these which are communicated to the newly-raised Master Mason in the third degree ceremony.

Once the Freemason has been raised to the degree of a Master Mason, normally at the following meeting, he will receive a Grand Lodge Certificate stating the dates of his initiation and raising. This certificate is used as a sort of 'Masonic passport' in that it will enable him to visit other lodges and is a proof that he has been raised to the degree of a Master Mason. When presented with his Grand Lodge Certificate, the recently raised Master Mason is warned not to display it in a frame or in other form. Grand Lodge Certificates, like the tracing boards, have evolved over time from the certificates originally issued by private lodges, going through several patterns before stabilising into more or less their current form after the Union in 1813. There are references to certificates being issued by private lodges in the early 1720s and they are mentioned explicitly in Anderson's Constitutions of 1738.

Whilst it is important to remember that Charity has always been a very important aspect of English Freemasonry (and remains so to this day) it would be incorrect to see Freemasonry as simply a type of Friendly Society. It is certainly true that early Grand Lodge Certificates were sometimes used by Freemasons in distress, or by their dependents, to petition relief from one of the Grand Lodges. There are many such instances recorded in the minute-books of both Grand Lodges. A very typical example from the National Archives in Kew is the petition of Mary Oliver, wife of Francis Oliver of the Ancient Union Lodge, No.203, in Liverpool, whose husband had failed to return from a sea-voyage to Jamaica. In general, once relief had been granted the certificate was destroyed. Perhaps not very surprisingly there are records of forged certificates being presented in fraudulent attempts to obtain alms. It has been argued that it might have been the burden of petitions for relief from itinerant Freemasons (in particular from Scottish and Irish Freemasons) which led to the Premier Grand Lodge reversing the first and second degree passwords, a move which was certainly one of the factors which led to the formation of the Antient Grand Lodge in 1751. After the Union in 1813, the United Grand Lodge banned the issue of certificates by private lodges and instead instituted a system of centrally-issued Grand Lodge Certificates, a ruling which is still in force today. Many of the symbols used on the current design may be found on the first degree tracing board, including the Doric, Ionic and Corinthian columns and the Rough and Perfect Ashlars. However, the certificate has no ritual function itself, although it is customary to include an explanation of its use and its symbolism when presenting it to a Master Mason at the meeting following his Raising.

Before the Union, both Grand Lodges had issued certificates in several different designs including a very attractive design in use by the Moderns of the Premier Grand Lodge which featured St. Paul's cathedral, perhaps emphasising again the importance of London to English Freemasonry at this time. Shortly before the Union, certificates issued by the Moderns featured the three Graces of Faith, Hope and Charity, whereas those of the Antients made more prominent use of the three pillars and most closely resemble the form used today.

For many Freemasons the third degree is their final step on the Masonic pathway, except perhaps for serving a term as Worshipful Master of their lodge. Some Freemasons find that it is only when committing entire ceremonies to memory as Worshipful Master that they start to acquire a better understanding of the ritual. In large lodges, a newly raised Master Mason may have to wait for several years before starting to progress through the offices leading to the Master's chair, which must include at least a whole year as a Warden, whereas in smaller lodges that progression may start much sooner. Election as Worshipful Master is by no means automatic however, and a Master Mason's progression may be delayed if it is felt by the other Past Masters that he is not yet ready.

The office of Worshipful Master is, according to the Emulation Ritual, 'the highest honour the lodge has in its power to confer on any of its members'. The Worshipful Master of the lodge acts as its head for the period of his term of office, during which time he will conduct the various degree ceremonies being worked. Many Freemasons only ever experience one year in office, with perhaps a second year much later in their Masonic careers, although in smaller lodges it is not uncommon for the Worshipful Master to be re-elected so that he serves a two-year term. No Master may serve more than two consecutive years in office without dispensation from the United Grand Lodge. This proscription may have developed from the early years of speculative Freemasonry in the eighteenth century when lodges frequently met in inns and ale-houses, and would have been intended to prevent pub landlords becoming the permanent Master of lodges meeting at their establishments.

The Installation ceremony has a mainly administrative function as it marks the start of the new Master's term of office and enables him to appoint and invest his officers. However, it does include a small section of esoteric ritual, which is restricted to the Master-elect and those members who are Past Masters, and which is known as the Inner Working. For most Freemasons the moment of being physically placed into the chair of his lodge by his immediate predecessor is one of the proudest and most memorable occasions in his Masonic career. The change in Masonic rank from Master Mason to Installed Master (and later, once his term in office has come to an end, as Past Master) has several practical effects. For example, he will qualify for membership, if he so wishes, of a Lodge of Installed Masters. Such lodges do not work degree ceremonies but often engage in Masonic research with the resulting papers being read out in open lodge. Although no longer the case, for many years Master Masons could not attend Grand Lodge unless they currently held the office of Warden, whereas installed Masters and Past Masters could attend by right; Master Masons can now attend when accompanied by a Past Master. Perhaps more significantly, until as recently as November 2004 no member of a Royal Arch chapter could be installed as one of its Principals without having previously been installed as the Worshipful Master of his Craft lodge. Indeed, in the very early days of Royal Arch Freemasonry only Installed Masters or Past Masters were even eligible for membership. One of the effects of this restriction was the creation of a ceremony of 'passing the veils'. This is not now conducted in English Freemasonry except as a demonstration, although it still forms a part of the progression to the Royal Arch degree as practised by other constitutions.

The Master's chair itself is a symbol of the office of Worshipful Master and is frequently referred to as the chair of King Solomon. The chair as a symbol of the head of the household has a very long history. In medieval and early Renaissance households there were very few chairs: most of the members of the household sat on benches or perhaps stools. Even today, sets of dining-room chairs are often sold with one 'carver's chair' which has arm-rests, although more recently two 'carvers' chairs' are perhaps more common. The Master's chair itself is therefore a symbolic throne. It is always placed, figuratively if not actually, at the East of the lodge room itself: the entrance to any lodge room is always towards the other 'western' end. Consequentially both the position and the size of the chair itself tend to dominate the ritual space of the lodge room. A fine example is lodge room No.10 in Freemasons' Hall in London where the Worshipful Master's chair and pedestal are flanked by imposing Egyptian columns.

It was not uncommon for older lodges to commission special chairs for the Worshipful Master and his Wardens. Typically the Master's chair will be much larger than the Wardens', reflecting the importance of the office of Worshipful Master. Freemasons' Hall in London has many examples belonging to the lodges that meet there, and there is even a set of chairs belonging to an Old School lodge, which rather charmingly appear to have been made from disused school-desks, complete with carved graffiti from the desk lids. Many of these Master's and Wardens' chairs are rather heavy and formal, emphasising the solemnity of the position of Worshipful Master, but this is by no means always the case. The Library and Museum of Freemasonry has a delightful example of a Master's chair made in the style of George Hepplewhite in the eighteenth century. Rather than the more usual, somewhat ponderous, throne-like design of many Master's chairs, this chair has a much lighter and more elegant design, even though it is very large at nearly two metres tall and almost a metre wide (**Fig. 30**). In use it may well have been even taller as there is a socket at the top of the cresting-rail where a banner may once have been inserted. The carved symbol on top of the cresting-rail is a beehive, representing industry, a symbol which no longer appears in current Masonic working.

The elegantly carved and pierced splat has small painted panels 'hanging' by carved ribbons from two flanking rosettes and a central swag. The central panel has a carved Square, the emblem of the Worshipful Master, and has the words 'Glory to God on High' painted on it. The panel to the left has a pair of Compasses resting on an arc with the Sun between the arms of the Compass, while the panel to the right has a Square, Level and Plumb Rule. The curved and downward-sweeping arms above the serpentine seat-rail and the straight neoclassical legs manage to combine a sense of strength with a lightness of touch which suggests its design may have been inspired by George Hepplewhite's *Cabinet Maker and Upholsterer's Guide* (1788-94). As is quite usual, this chair forms part of a set of three chairs; the other two (somewhat smaller) chairs are for the Senior and Junior Wardens and are carved with the emblems of their offices.

Even though the large size of many of these chairs is a reflection of the importance of the office itself, there may also have been more practical considerations. Amongst the most famous Masonic chairs made at the end of the eighteenth century are the now

ABOVE **Fig.30: Mahogany Master's Chair in the style of George Hepplewhite with Masonic emblems, c.1780.** *Image © The Library and Museum of Freemasonry, London.*

heavily-restored thrones made by Robert Kennett in 1791 following the election of the Prince of Wales (later George IV) as Grand Master of the Premier Grand Lodge in 1790. The Grand Master's chair is enormous, and even bearing in mind its symbolic significance there is no doubt that the Prince of Wales' huge bulk would have filled it.

It is rare, although by no means unheard of, for a Freemason never to be installed as Master of his lodge, although the vast majority of Freemasons will at some point in their Masonic career spend a year in the chair of their lodge. However, it is also true that the majority of Freemasons never progress further than the three Craft degrees, even though it is made clear to every Master Mason that their Masonic journey is incomplete and the possession of the third degree's 'substituted secrets' is insufficient. Although not the majority, a very sizeable minority of Master Masons (approximately forty per cent) will seek to complete their main Masonic journey. For these Freemasons, the next step is to be 'exalted' into a Royal Arch chapter.

The Royal Arch degree is not the only other 'higher degree' or 'side degree' but it is probably the most popular, and membership of it is required for some other degrees, such as the Knights Templar. Most importantly, in English Freemasonry, it is the only 'higher degree' administered by the United Grand Lodge; indeed it is seen as an essential component of 'pure antient Freemasonry'.

For many years the Royal Arch degree was described explicitly as being the Master Mason's degree completed, and not a separate fourth degree. However, in December 2003, the reality of the situation was finally accepted and the Royal Arch degree was recognised by the United Grand Lodge as being a separate order. This somewhat confused situation originated as the result of a compromise reached at the time of the Union in 1813. Together with the transposition of the signs of recognition between the first and second degrees, the position of the Royal Arch degree had been one of the major causes of the schism in English Freemasonry, which led to the creation of the Antient Grand Lodge in 1751. The Moderns of the Premier Grand Lodge had no taste for the Royal Arch and even as late as 1792 had resolved to have nothing to do with the 'Society of Royal Arch Masons'. For the Antients, however, the Royal Arch was an essential part of Freemasonry.

The Royal Arch ritual is based on another Old Testament narrative: the return of the Israelites to Jerusalem after their captivity in Babylon and the rebuilding of the great temple at Jerusalem. During the rebuilding three workmen, described in the ritual as 'sojourners', discover a hidden vault in the ruins of the old temple. The candidate represents one of the sojourners, and during a rather dramatic part of the ceremony is figuratively lowered into the vault where the secrets lost by the murder of Hiram Abiff in the third degree are recovered. The second part of the ceremony contains three lectures examining in turn the historical, symbolical and mystical aspects of the ceremony.

Because of the rather dramatic content of the Royal Arch ceremony itself tracing boards are not really needed to illustrate the ritual, although John Harris nonetheless produced two different boards in 1844 (**Figs. 31 & 32**). One depicts the layout of the chapter room itself, displaying minor differences to current practice. The second board shows the narrative of the Royal Arch legend itself.

The board illustrating the legend of the Royal Arch degree depicts many of the elements of the story of the exaltation ceremony. The ruins of the first temple at Jerusalem are shown with Egyptian-style columns while the city of Jerusalem visible behind the building site reflects, perhaps incongruously, a medieval European style of architecture. The veiled double-cube of the altar of incense is surrounded by symbols of the Zodiac, which do not feature in Masonic ritual, even though they may be found on the walls of Grand Temple in Freemasons' Hall in London. Although presented as a single image the discovery of the vault's roof arch and the abandoned tools of the sojourners do not belong to the same narrative space as the view of the vault itself. The composition, however, successfully distracts the viewer from the difference in vantage-points and effectively represents the narrative of the ritual.

The second board depicts the layout of a chapter room, which is very different to that of a lodge room. The twelve banners of the tribes of Israel surround the central carpet, which has as its main focus the veiled altar of incense, the unveiling of which is one of the most significant moments of the ceremony. The triangle towards the rear is formed by the sceptres carried by each of the three Principals as part of their regalia. In Royal Arch Freemasonry, the three principals sit on a dais at the far end of the chapter room. This practice reflects early craft working when the Senior and Junior Wardens used to sit flanking the Worshipful Master, rather than having their own pedestals in the West and South as they do today.

At the back of the dais are four banners depicting an ox, a lion, a man and an eagle. Each banner not only represents one of the four divisions of the army of Israel, but also has additional meanings, which are explained in the Royal Arch ritual. The ox represents patience, the lion symbolises strength, the man personifies intelligence and the eagle the speed at which the Will of God is executed. However, it is possible that before the

ABOVE **Fig.31: John Harris, Royal Arch Tracing Board, showing the legend of the ritual story, 1844.** *Image © The Library and Museum of Freemasonry, London.*

ABOVE **Fig. 32: John Harris, Royal Arch Tracing Board showing the layout of a chapter room, 1844.** *Image © The Library and Museum of Freemasonry, London.*

de-Christianisation of the Craft and the Royal Arch these may well have represented St. Mark (lion), St. Luke (ox), St. Matthew (man) and St. John (eagle) as would have been normal in more explicitly religious works of art. The ox, lion, man and eagle also formed the arms of the Antient Grand Lodge, which is perhaps an indication of the importance of the Royal Arch ritual to the Antient Grand Lodge. The central banner shows the Triple Tau, the symbol of the Royal Arch order itself. The design of a chapter room today is not significantly different from Harris' design apart from the addition of five Platonic bodies which are discussed in older versions of the Symbolical lecture delivered as part of the exaltation ceremony and are said to represent the four elements and the sphere of the Universe.

Neither of these tracing board designs ever gained as much popularity as Harris' Craft designs did, perhaps because they were superfluous to Royal Arch ritual. The board depicting the design of the chapter room merely replicated what the candidate could actually see in front of him. In the Craft ceremonies, the tracing boards could be used to point out various symbols, whilst in the Royal Arch ceremony the symbols being explained, especially in the Symbolical Lecture, are already present in the chapter room and are indicated directly by the Second Principal who delivers the lecture. Even though these designs were not widely adopted they were nevertheless still being advertised for sale in *Spencer's Masonic Depot* in the 1870s.

Initially, admission to the Royal Arch degree was only open to those who had previously been installed as Worshipful Master of their lodges, which could in some cases lead to a considerable delay before being exalted. In response to this, many Antients lodges used a ceremony of 'passing the chair' in which the Master Mason underwent almost exactly the same ritual as an installation, but after a few moments seated on the Worshipful Master's chair he would then be politely asked to vacate it before receiving his Past Master's collar jewel.

Such was the importance of the Royal Arch degree to the Antients, that its inclusion within the newly United Grand Lodge was essential. To this day the Book of Constitutions of United Grand Lodge states in its preliminary declaration that 'pure Antient Masonry consists of three degrees and no more, *viz.* those of the Entered Apprentice, the Fellowcraft and the Master Mason, including the Supreme Order of the Holy Royal Arch'.

In the Craft degrees the Freemason is presented with practical guidance on how to live a more upright and moral life. The more spiritual side of his nature is only briefly explored during the third degree ceremony, when the ritual leads him to consider his own inevitable death. The Royal Arch degree's importance is that it develops these ideas of spirituality and provides a framework for the Royal Arch Freemason to contemplate his own deeper spirituality. In no sense does this framework replace any of his own religious beliefs; on the contrary, Freemasonry is essentially a set of tools, which should enable him to understand, appreciate and ultimately reinforce his own beliefs.

The revelation at the heart of Royal Arch Freemasonry and, by extension, the Craft itself is therefore one of spirituality: that man is not only fundamentally a spiritual being but needs to possess an understanding of the nature of the Supreme Being. As Klein wrote in 1912, it is 'a knowledge of our Spiritual Environment which alone can bring us into sympathy with the Great Reality'. Most importantly, the precise nature of this personal concept of the Supreme Being will depend on the religious or spiritual beliefs of each individual member, which is why, in the English constitution at least, atheists may not be initiated as Freemasons or even visit overseas lodges which operate under Grand Lodges, which do admit atheists. Ultimately, by denying the existence of any kind of Supreme Being, the atheist also denies the spiritual nature of man.

Once the Freemason has been exalted into the Royal Arch and has perhaps been installed as Worshipful Master of his lodge and in turn similarly as Third, Second and First Principal of his chapter, it would seem that part of his Masonic journey will be complete. That is to say, having been initiated as an Entered Apprentice he will have ascended the Winding Staircase of the Fellowcraft by devoting time to education and learning. In the third degree he will have contemplated his mortality and should he have chosen to be exalted into the Royal Arch he will have had the opportunity to gain a better understanding of the nature of his spirituality and his faith.

The rest of the Freemason's journey will naturally unfold over the course of the rest of his life; however, it can be argued that he will now possess the equipment he needs to deal more easily with the inevitable challenges he will face. In the same way that operative stonemasons use their tools to create strong, useful and beautiful buildings, so the vocabulary of Freemasonry uses the symbols of design, construction and measurement to create a spiritual framework which will enable the thoughtful Freemason to be more grounded, both in who he is and what he believes in. It would be quite wrong to suggest that the spiritual pathway of self-discovery which the symbols and allegories of Freemasonry make available to its members is particularly well trodden. Some critics of Freemasonry might argue that this notion of spirituality is nothing new and, indeed is no different from the teachings of many religions: in a sense therefore, Freemasonry is pointless. Ironically, this criticism itself would seem to be missing the point. The tools are there, but it is not compulsory to use them.

The symbols and allegories of Freemasonry are not a substitute for a Freemason's own religious beliefs: rather they enable him to go through a process of self-examination and self-discovery and ultimately make sense of his place in both the world he lives in and the world of his faith.

CONCLUSION

In the initiation ceremony, the new Freemason is informed that Freemasonry is based on three fundamental principles of Brotherly Love, Relief and Truth. The importance of charity is stressed during the ceremony as the new member is reminded that misfortune can affect us all. Every lodge meeting sees charitable collections and, with additional contributions to lodge benevolent funds, substantial amounts are raised each year from the membership: indeed the combined totals of the funds administered by the Masonic Charities in England and Wales in 2006-7 amounted to nearly £299 million, making it then the 24th largest charity in the UK.

It is certainly true that many Freemasons see Freemasonry as nothing more than an enjoyable hobby. The same critics who described Freemasonry as 'pointless' went on to describe it as 'little more than a social club providing an opportunity to indulge in some amateur theatricals followed by a meal and plenty of beer'. There are undoubtedly many Freemasons who might be described as 'knife and fork Masons'; for them, the most important part of a Masonic evening is the Festive Board, as indeed it was for many eighteenth-century Freemasons. Yet the fact remains that they have chosen to become Freemasons rather than join, say, Round Table or a Rotary club.

Although most private lodges tend to attract a somewhat homogeneous membership – after all, most of their new members are introduced by their current members – Freemasonry does cut across lines of social distinction and the idea of equality stretches back to the earliest days of Craft Freemasonry when highly educated gentlemen like Elias Ashmole sought out the company of educated stonemasons. Even from its early days, Freemasonry appealed to men of different social standing. One of the more recent acquisitions of the Library and Museum of Freemasonry is a delightful model of a military lodge meeting which has been placed in a bottle (**Fig. 33**).

This charming military lodge meeting in a bottle probably dates from the late eighteenth century. The soldiers all have queued and clubbed hair and the shortened red coats with lengthened lapels, white facings and gold lace suggest a cavalry regiment, as do the chevron cuffs and lace. The Worshipful Master, who is standing beneath an arch covered with foliage and Masonic symbols, has bright red hair. From the rear it appears that he not only has very short legs but is standing on a box to give him greater height, suggesting that there might possibly be a satirical element to the composition and that the Worshipful Master figure could even represent a real person. The five men are all wearing very large aprons, rather than the smaller ones favoured in the nineteenth century.

Small tableaux in bottles are a form of folk art, which began to appear in the early eighteenth century as the technology to make clear glass was developed. Ships in bottles are probably the most well-known examples, although some of the very earliest examples depict places of work such as mine-workings. Unlike the rest of the objects discussed in this book, the *Lodge Meeting in a Bottle* serves no ritual purpose and is emphatically a private object. The creation of such models was a very laborious and time-consuming craft and would have required a great deal of patience. The maker of the *Lodge Meeting in a Bottle* clearly felt that this was a worthwhile and meaningful task: he undoubtedly had first-hand knowledge of both the army and

ABOVE **Fig 33: Lodge Meeting in a Bottle, probably late eighteenth century.** *Image © Painton Cowan and The Library and Museum of Freemasonry, London.*

Masonic practice at the time and has created a delightful tableau, which strikes a chord with the modern Freemason.

The folk art nature of the *Lodge Meeting in a Bottle* and the fact that the lodge members are from the ranks at a time when the leadership of both Grand Lodges was aristocratic is indicative of Freemasonry's appeal across a broad section of society.

All Freemasons meet as equals: their religion, race and socio-economic situations are irrelevant as they pursue their shared spiritual journey through life. The rituals and ceremonies of Freemasonry serve to create a bond amongst its members, as every new member will be aware that every single person in the lodge room will, at some time have gone through the same ceremony: the title 'brother' is not one that is bestowed lightly.

What makes Freemasonry so special is that, over its three-hundred-year history, its remarkable vocabulary of symbolism and allegory have developed into a system which not only encourages good citizenship, honesty and integrity but can also lead the Freemason on an extremely rewarding journey of self-discovery and spiritual awareness, in company with others who consciously and conscientiously pursue the same path.

In modern Freemasonry there is, perhaps, a tendency to concentrate on the words of the rituals and their delivery within the lodge room; however, the symbols and imagery of the Craft are central to the lessons it seeks to convey. The depiction of these symbols has evolved from the earliest diagrams drawn on the floor of the lodge room in chalk or charcoal into ritual objects, which possess not only deep meaning but also at times, great beauty. It is not only in the ritual practices of Freemasonry that we may find traces of the medieval stonemason. The artistry they displayed in building the great cathedrals has echoes that are more intimate in the sometimes beautiful, but always meaningful, symbolic art of Masonic imagery.

GLOSSARY

Acacia: an aromatic plant associated with grave markings.

Accepted: initiated or adopted into the Order.

Acception: an inner circle of the London Company of Masons, active in the late seventeenth century, possibly a precursor of speculative Freemasonry.

All-Seeing Eye: a symbol of the Supreme Being, also described in Freemasonry as the *Great Architect Of The Universe* (GAOTU).

Ancient and Accepted Rite: a rite of thirty-three degrees of which the three Craft degrees are counted as being the first three. In England the only degree worked in private chapters is the eighteenth degree, often referred to as Rose Croix; also known as Scottish Rite Masonry or Ecossais, from the French.

Ancient Craft Masonry: the degrees of Entered Apprentice, Fellowcraft and Master Mason.

Anno Lucis: in the Year of Light, preceding Anno Domini by 4,000 years.

Antients: Freemasons with allegiance to the second Grand Lodge formed in London in 1751, so called after their insistence that they alone practised 'pure antient masonry' as opposed to those with allegiance to the Premier Grand Lodge, whose adherents were termed 'Moderns' because of their adoption of new Masonic practices.

Apron: the main item of regalia of a Freemason. The Entered Apprentice apron is of pure white lambskin. The Fellowcraft's bears two light-blue rosettes. The Master Mason's apron has a light-blue border and three light-blue rosettes. On being installed as Worshipful Master, the rosettes are exchanged for levels.

Ashlar: a block of stone, see Rough Ashlar and Perfect Ashlar.

Blazing Star: according to the *Lectures* a symbol representing the Sun but also understood as a symbol for the Supreme Being.

Boaz: the name of one of the pillars at the entrance of King Solomon's Temple. Its Masonic meaning is 'Strength'. It features in both the first and second degree ceremonies.

Brother: a member of a Craft lodge.

Chapiter: an architectural term referring to the capital of a column.

Chapter: the Royal Arch equivalent of a lodge. Also used by some other higher degree bodies.

Charge: an oration setting out duties and responsibilities. The Old Charges, possibly dating from the fourteenth century, have evolved into the Laws of Craft Masonry as set out in the Book of Constitutions.

Chequered Pavement: see Mosaic Pavement.

Chisel: a Masonic tool used to smooth the Rough Ashlar. Its symbolic meaning is 'Education'.

Column: the architectural uprights supporting the entablature.

Companion: a member of a Royal Arch chapter. A term of address for a Royal Arch Mason.

Compasses: an architectural and Masonic implement, representing 'Virtue' and used as a symbolic tool to control passion.

Crow: a crowbar used as a lever to lift heavy stones. It features significantly in Royal Arch ritual.

Deacon: there are two deacons within each lodge, one senior and one junior. The office forms part of the progression towards the Master's chair. Deacons conduct the perambulations of candidates during the three degree ceremonies of Craft Freemasonry.

Double Cube: a solid the size of two cubes, one placed on top of the other. A double-cube serves as an altar of incense in the Royal Arch ritual.

Ecossais: the French word meaning 'Scottish', often used in conjunction with a form of 'higher degree' Freemasonry known more usually as the Ancient and Accepted Rite.

Emulation Ritual: the ritual practice promulgated by the Emulation Lodge of Improvement, one of the main bodies set up to ensure that Masonic ritual remains pure and unchanged by inadvertent incremental changes.

Entered Apprentice: the first degree of Craft Freemasonry. Entered Apprentices wear a pure white apron, generally made of lambskin, as their regalia.

Ephraimites: one of the tribes of Israel who were defeated by another tribe, the Gileadites, led by their General Jephthah. When the Ephraimites attempted to escape across the River Jordan their accent betrayed them and they were slain (Judges 12: 5-6). This legend is often featured on second degree tracing boards.

Exaltation: the ceremony of initiation into a Royal Arch chapter.

Ezra: the name of a scribe in Royal Arch Freemasonry. Scribe Ezra is the equivalent Royal Arch office to Secretary in a Craft lodge.

Fellowcraft: the second degree in Craft Freemasonry. Fellowcraft Freemasons wear an apron of white lambskin with two light-blue rosettes as their regalia.

Festive Board: a supper or dinner eaten after a lodge or chapter meeting.

First Principal: in Royal Arch Masonry, the equivalent office to that of Worshipful Master in a Craft lodge. The name of the office is Zerubbabel.

Floorcloth: a precursor to the Tracing Boards. A cloth placed on the floor of the lodge room on which Masonic symbols have been marked.

Freemason: formerly a skilled worker in stone who had served a full apprenticeship, now more usually applied to a member of the Fraternity of Free and Accepted Masons.

Gauge: a tool of measurement, most usually a twenty-four inch ruler used to measure length but also used symbolically to point out the twenty-four hours of the day and how they should be spent.

Gavel: a stonemason's hammer, often used with a chisel to remove lumps from rough stone. Also a symbol of authority for the Worshipful Master and the Senior and Junior Wardens.

Geometry: one of the Seven Liberal Arts and Sciences, it enables figures to be drawn in precise relationship to each other. The science of Geometry is of fundamental importance to architecture as it determines how angles and lengths may be measured.

Gileadites: one of the tribes of Israel who, led by their General Jephthah, defeated another tribe, the Ephraimites. When the latter attempted to escape across the River Jordan, their accent betrayed them and they were slain (Judges 12: 5-6). This legend is often featured on second degree tracing boards.

Gormagons: an order of pseudo-Freemasons allegedly created by the Duke of Wharton in London in the 1720s but in all probability a hoax.

Grand Geometrician of the Universe: a term used to refer to the Supreme Being in the second degree of Craft Freemasonry. In the first and third degrees the Supreme Being is referred to as the Great Architect of the Universe and in the Royal Arch as The True and Living God Most High.

Grand Master: the Head of a Grand Lodge.

Grand Steward: an officer of Grand Lodge whose duty is to accompany the Grand Master or his representative as an honour guard.

Grand Tyler: the Tyler of Grand Lodge.

Great Architect of the Universe: a term used to refer to the Supreme Being used in the first and third degrees of Craft Masonry. It is an expression which is acceptable to Freemasons of any faith. In the second degree the Supreme Being is referred to as the Grand Geometrician of the Universe and in the Royal Arch as The True and Living God Most High.

Greater Lights, Three: the Volume of the Sacred Law, the Square and Compasses. In the first degree both points of the Compasses lie underneath the Square. In the second degree one point is disclosed. In the third degree both points are shown, implying that the new Master Mason is free to work without restrictions with his new-found knowledge and wisdom.

Grip: a handshake.

Haggai: the name of the office of Second Principal in a Royal Arch chapter.

Higher Degrees: other degrees of Freemasonry beyond those of Craft Freemasonry, all of which demand the rank of Master Mason in the Craft as a minimum entry requirement. Popular higher degrees other than the Royal Arch include the Ancient and Accepted Rite (or Rose Croix) and Mark Masonry.

Hiram Abiff: the chief architect of King Solomon's Temple in Jerusalem, whose death at the hands of treacherous Fellowcrafts forms the basis of the third degree Ceremony.

Hiram King of Tyre: one of the three original Grand Masters, the others being King Solomon and Hiram Abiff.

Holy Royal Arch: a 'higher degree' of Freemasonry. It is very closely linked to Craft Freemasonry and is widely considered to be an essential part of the Masonic journey. It is the only such degree explicitly recognised by the United Grand Lodge of England.

Inner Guard: an officer in a Craft lodge who is responsible for admitting latecomers and candidates. Typically the first ritually-active office of the progression ladder to the Master's chair.

Jachin: the name of a pillar at the entrance of King Solomon's Temple. Its Masonic meaning is 'To Establish'. It features in the second and third degree ceremonies.

Jacob's Ladder: featured on the first degree tracing board, it represents the path to Heaven. Typically it will include the symbols of a cross, an anchor and a heart representing the Christian theological virtues of Faith, Hope and Charity. They are sometimes represented with three female figures, one of which (Charity) is usually accompanied by a child.

Janitor: the equivalent of Tyler in a Royal Arch chapter.

Jephthah: the General commanding the Gileadites who defeated the invading

Ephraimites. This legend is often featured on second degree tracing boards.

Jewel: an emblem of office worn on a collar by the officers of a lodge or chapter. A breast-jewel is worn by past masters of a lodge or chapter and a different breast-jewel forms part of Royal Arch regalia.

Joshua: the name of the office of Third Principal in a Royal Arch chapter.

Junior Warden: a senior officer of a private lodge, third in seniority behind the Worshipful Master and the Senior Warden.

Keystone: the stone at the top of an arch which binds it together. The Keystone features heavily in the ritual drama of both the Royal Arch and Mark Masonry.

Lesser Lights, Three: the Sun, Moon and the Master of the lodge.

Level: an operative stonemason's tool used to check that all horizontal surfaces are truly level. It represents 'Equality' and is worn on the collar of the Junior Warden as the jewel of his office.

Lewis: a set of wedge-shaped metal plates, which can be inserted into a suitable cavity on the top of a block of stone. Under tension they enable the block to be lifted into place by a hoist or derrick. The uninitiated son of a Freemason is also known as a Lewis.

Lily-work: a form of embellishment on the capitals of the pillars at the entrance to King Solomon's temple. Its meaning is 'Peace'.

Lodge: a club of Freemasons.

Mahabone: an exclamation uttered by characters featured in the Traditional History from the third degree ritual, when discovering the body of the murdered Chief Architect, Hiram Abiff.

Mark Masonry: a popular 'higher degree' of Freemasonry. It is not recognised as a degree of Craft Freemasonry by the United Grand Lodge of England. Its emblem is a Keystone.

Master Mason: the third degree in Freemasonry. Not to be confused with the Master of the lodge who must, however, be at least a Master Mason in rank. Master Masons typically progress through the offices of the lodge to become Master in due course.

Maul: an operative stonemason's tool used as a hammer with the chisel. It represents 'Conscience' and plays an important role in the third degree ceremony.

Moderns: Freemasons owing allegiance to the first or Premier Grand Lodge before the Union. So called by the 'Antients' due to the latter's belief that the Moderns favoured inappropriate ritual innovations.

Moon: one of the Three Lesser Lights, the Moon rules the night and is represented in the lodge by the Senior Warden, who closes the lodge when the work is completed.

Mosaic Pavement: the chequered flooring inside King Solomon's Temple. Its black and white squares symbolise night and day, good and evil.

Nehemiah: the name of a scribe in Royal Arch Freemasonry. Scribe Nehemiah has a similar role to the Inner Guard in a Craft lodge, but is a more important office.

Net-work: a form of embellishment on the capitals of the pillars at the entrance to King Solomon's temple. Its meaning is 'Unity'.

Obligation: a solemn oath sworn by candidates on the book they hold most holy to abide by the laws and regulations of both United Grand Lodge and Supreme Grand Chapter and to keep confidential the Masonic secrets disclosed to them.

Operative: concerning stonemasons engaged in the physical craft of working with stone.

Past Master: a Freemason who has been Worshipful Master of his lodge.

Perfect Ashlar: a block of stone after it has been worked by the mason to be a perfectly smoothed building block. It represents the Master Mason.

Pickaxe: a mason's tool, which features in the Royal Arch ritual.

Pillar: a free-standing column which does not support an entablature. The pillars at the entrance to King Solomon's Temple feature in the first and second degree ceremonies.

Platonic bodies: solids referred to in Royal Arch ritual. They are probably quite a late addition to Royal Arch ritual and are placed on the floor of a Royal Arch chapter.

Plumb Rule: an operative stonemason's tool used to check that all upright surfaces are truly upright. It represents the just and upright conduct of a Freemason in his daily life. It is worn on the collar of the Junior Warden as the jewel of his office.

Point within a circle: a geometric design with many meanings. A point within a circle is a point from which a Freemason cannot move as he is bound by his duty, represented by the Circle. It may also symbolise the Supreme Being, orbited by the Sun.

Pomegranates: a form of embellishment on the capitals of the pillars at the entrance to King Solomon's temple. Their meaning is 'plenty'.

Premier Grand Lodge: the first Grand Lodge, established at the Goose and Gridiron Ale-house in London in 1717.

Principal: the three leading officers in a Royal Arch chapter are the First, Second and Third Principals.

Principal Sojourner: an officer in a Royal Arch chapter who conducts the candidate through much of the Royal Arch ceremony of Exaltation and is a leading character in the ritual drama of the degree.

Rough Ashlar: a rough-hewn block of stone newly arrived from the quarry, representing the newly initiated Entered Apprentice: of approximately the right shape but unformed and unfinished.

Royal Arch Masonry: see Holy Royal Arch.

Sanctum Sanctorum: the central chamber of the Temple at Jerusalem, the holiest of holy shrines.

Sanhedrin: an advisory council, which features in the Royal Arch ritual drama.

Scottish Masonry: often a reference to the 'higher degrees' of the Ancient and Accepted Rite (or Rose Croix) rather than a reference to Craft Freemasonry as practised in Scotland.

Scribe: an office in a Royal Arch chapter. See Scribe Ezra and Scribe Nehemiah.

Second Principal: in Royal Arch Masonry, the equivalent office to that of Senior Warden Master in a Craft lodge. The name of the office is Haggai.

Senior Grand Warden: a senior officer of Grand Lodge.

Senior Warden: in a private lodge the Senior Warden is second in importance only to the Worshipful Master.

Seven Liberal Arts and Sciences: the subjects considered essential for a classical education were: Grammar, Rhetoric, Logic, Arithmetic, Geometry, Music and Astronomy.

Shibboleth: a test word used by Jephthah's soldiers during the battle against the Ephraimites as described in the ritual of the second degree.

Skirret: an operative tool used to mark out a building's outline. One of the working tools of the third degree it may be a post-Union addition to the ritual.

Sojourner: the name of an office in a Royal Arch chapter. There are three Sojourners in a Royal Arch chapter. During the ceremony of Exaltation the candidate will play the role of one of the Sojourners.

Solomon: King Solomon was the most senior of the three original Grand Masters of Craft Freemasonry, the others being Hiram, King of Tyre and Hiram Abiff.

Speculative: a term to distinguish Masonic ritual practice from that of operative stonemasons who physically work with stone.

Square: an operative stonemason's tool used to check that right angles are true and square. It also represents 'Morality' and is a key symbol in speculative Freemasonry.

The Square is the symbol worn by the Worshipful Master of a lodge on his collar as part of his regalia.

Steward: an officer in a lodge with no ritual function. Their main function is to ensure wine glasses are kept full at the Festive Board.

Sun: one of the Three Lesser Lights, the Sun rules the day and is represented at its meridian by the Junior Warden in the lodge.

Tassels: found at each corner of the first degree tracing board symbolising the Four Cardinal Virtues of Fortitude, Temperance, Justice and Mercy.

Tessellated border: design motif at the edge of the lodge carpet and at the edges of the tracing boards. The tessellations symbolise the planets orbiting the Sun.

Third Principal: in Royal Arch Masonry, the equivalent office to that of Junior Warden in a Craft lodge. The name of the office is Joshua.

Tracing Board: in speculative Freemasonry, they are images illustrating elements of the ritual ceremonies of Craft Freemasonry. Much of the symbolism of Freemasonry is depicted on the tracing boards which form an important part of lodge furniture. See also 'True' Tracing Board.

Triple Tau: the emblem of Royal Arch Masonry formed by a triangular arrangement of three Greek letter Taus.

True and Living God Most High, The: a term used to refer to the Supreme Being used in Royal Arch Masonry.

True Tracing Board: a board used by operative stonemasons to draw plans and designs. It features on the first degree Tracing Board and refers to the Volume of the Sacred Law, which contains the Supreme Being's plans for mankind.

Tubal-Cain: a word featured in the third degree ceremony meaning 'Worldly Possessions'.

Twenty-Four Inch Gauge: an operative stonemason's tool used to measure length. It represents the twenty-four hours of the day and reminds Freemasons of how they should make proper use of the day.

Tyler: a Tyler acts as an outer guard during lodge meetings: he waits outside the door of the lodge room, prepares candidates and prevents intruders from disturbing the meeting. It is generally part of his duties to prepare the lodge room.

Vanitas Paintings: non-Masonic still-life paintings depicting symbols of mortality referring to the fleeting nature of human existence. Typical symbols include skulls, candles and hour-glasses.

Vault: a chamber, normally underneath a building. A vault features significantly in the Royal Arch ritual.

Volume of the Sacred Law: the writings held most sacred by a Freemason in his personal belief system. The lodge or chapter will display the book or writings held most sacred by the majority of its members, but candidates will always take their obligations on the book they consider most holy.

Warden: the two Wardens, Senior and Junior are the two most senior officers of a private lodge after the Worshipful Master. They have significant roles to play in all of the ritual dramas of the degree ceremonies.

Working: the name of the form of ritual, which is used by each lodge or chapter. The most commonly used ritual for Craft lodges is Emulation working. Others include Taylor's, Logic, Universal and Stability. The most commonly used Royal Arch working is Aldersgate.

Working Tools: in each of the three degrees of Craft Freemasonry, three sets of three operative stonemasons' tools are explained to the candidate, each tool having a practical use and a symbolic meaning.

Worshipful Master: the chairman and elected head of a lodge. One of the Three Lesser Lights, the Master rules the lodge.

Zerubbabel: the name of the office of First Principal in a Royal Arch chapter, equivalent to Worshipful Master in a Craft lodge.

BIBLIOGRAPHY

Aldersgate Chapter of Improvement. *Aldersgate Royal Arch Ritual.* Hersham: Lewis Masonic, 2005.

—. *Aldersgate Royal Arch Ritual.* Shepperton: Lewis Masonic, 1989.

Anderson, James. *The Constitutions of the Free-Masons containing the History, Charges, Regulations & c. of that most Ancient and Right Worshipful Fraternity.* London, 1723.

Association of Atholl Lodges. *Atholl Lodge List.* 2009. http://www.antients.co.uk/Lodge%20List.htm (accessed August 11, 2013).

Beck, Guy L. "Celestial Lodge Above: The Temple of Solomon in Jerusalem as a Religious Symbol in Freemasonry." *Nova Religio: The Journal of Alternative and Emergent Religions, Vol. 4, No 1*, October 2000: 28-51.

Beresiner, Yasha. "William Hogarth: Portrait of a Mason-Artist." *MQ Magazine.* October 2003. http://www.mqmagazine.co.uk/issue-7/p-07.php (accessed July 8, 2013).

Berman, Ric. *The Foundations of Modern Freemasonry.* Eastbourne: Sussex Academic Press, 2012.

Burr, Erastus. *Grand Chapter of Royal Arch Masons of Alberta: The Royal Arch Floor Cloth.* 2009. http://www.royalarchmasonsalberta.com/index.php/library/aspeslet-library/ram/153-the-royal-arch-floor-cloth (accessed August 1, 2013).

Calderwood, Paul. *Freemasonry and the Press in the Twentieth Century.* Farnham: Ashgate Publishing Ltd., 2013.

Cherry, Martin. *The Six Masonic Sons of George III, Part 2, Augustus Frederick, Duke of Sussex.* April 2005. http://www.mqmagazine.co.uk/issue-13/p-20.php (accessed February 3, 2013).

Cryer, Rev'd Neville Barker. *The Royal Arch Journey.* Hersham: Lewis Masonic, 2009.

Curl, James Stevens. *The Art and Architecture of Freemasonry.* London: B.T. Batsford Ltd, 1991.

de Hoyos, Arturo (ed), and S Brent Morris (ed). *Freemasonry in Context: History, Ritual, Controversy.* Lanham: Lexington Books, 2004.

de Pace, M. *Introducing Freemasonry.* Shepperton: Lewis Masonic, 1983.

Dring, E. H. "The Evolution and Development of the Tracing or Lodge Board." *Ars Quatuor Coronatorum Vol. XXIX*, 1916: 243-264; 274-326.

Dyer, Colin. *Symbolism in Craft Freemasonry.* Hersham: Lewis Masonic, 2003.

Elliott, Paul, and Stephen Daniels. "The 'School of True, Useful and Universal Science'? Freemasonry, Natural Philosophy and Scientific Culture in Eighteenth-Century England." *The British Journal for the History of Science, Vol. 39, No.2,* June 2006: 207-229.

Emulation Lodge of Improvement. *Emulation Ritual.* Shepperton: Lewis (Masonic Publishers) Limited, 1986.

—. *The Lectures of the Three Degrees in Craft Masonry.* Shepperton: Lewis (Masonic Publishers) Limited, 1974.

Francis, George. "Out of the Shadows." *Freemasonry Today*, Summer 2013: 41-43.

Gist, Noel P. "Culture Patterning in Secret Society Ceremonials." *Social Forces Vol.14 No.4,* May 1936: 497-505.

Hallett, Mark. *Hogarth.* London: Phaidon Press, 2000.

Hallett, Mark, and Christine Riding. *Hogarth.* London: Tate Publishing, 2007.

Haunch, Terence Osborne. "English Craft Certificates." *Ars Quatuor Coronatorum Vol. LXXXII*, 1969.

—. *Freemasons' Hall, The Home and Heritage of the Craft.* London: The United Grand Lodge of England, 1983.

—. *Tracing Boards, their development and their designers.* Rochester: Hamilton House, 1976.

Henderson, Kent. *Masonic World Guide.* Shepperton: Lewis Masonic, 1984.

Hughan, W.J. "Old Tracing Boards." *Masonic Illustrated,* (January) 1903: 85.

Iliffe, Rob, and Michael Hawkins. *The Newton Project.* 2013. http://www.newtonproject.sussex.ac.uk/prism.php?id=1 (accessed July 8, 2013).

Jackson, A.C.F. *A Glossary of the Craft and Holy Royal Arch Rituals of Freemasonry.* Addlestone: Lewis Masonic, 1992.

—. *Rose Croix: The History of the Ancient and Accepted Rite for England and Wales.* Shepperton: Lewis Masonic, 1987.

Jackson, Keith. *Beyond the Craft.* Shepperton: Lewis Masonic, 1982.

Klein, Sydney. "Hidden Mystery No.VII, The Real Personality or Transcendental Ego." *Ars Quatuor Coronatorum Vol. XXV*, 1912: 285-301.

Knight, Christopher, and Robert Lomas. *The Hiram Key: Pharaohs,Freemasons and the Discovery of the Secret Scrolls of Jesus.* London: Century Books, 1996.

MacNulty, W. Kirk. *Freemasonry: A Journey through Ritual and Symbol.* London: Thames and Hudson Ltd., 1991.

—. *Freemasonry: Symbols, Secrets, Significance.* London: Thames and Hudson, 2006.

Moore, Duncan. *A Guide to Masonic Symbolism*. Hersham : Lewis Masonic, 2009.
Pick, Fred L, and G Norman Knight. *The Pocket History of Freemasonry.* London: Frederick Muller Limited, 1991.
Pink, Andrew. "A Music Club for Freemasons: Philo-Musicae et Architecturae Societas Apollini, London, 1725-1727." *Early Music*, Vol. 39 Issue 10. 2010.
Rees, Julian. *Making Light: A Handbook for Freemasons*. Hersham: Lewis Masonic, 2006.
—. *The Stairway of Freemasonry.* Hersham: Lewis Masonic, 2007.
—. *Tracing Boards of the Three Degrees of Craft Masonry Explained*. Hersham: Lewis Masonic, 2009 .
Rylands, W. H. "Hogarth's Night." *Ars Quatuor Coronatorum Vol. II*, 1889: 116-117.
—. "The Masonic Apron." *Ars Quatuor Coronatorum Vol. V*, 1892: 172-191.
Sadler, Henry. "Tracing Boards of Lodge No.262." *Masonic Illustrated*, (May) 1901: 172-3.
Sloan (Ed.), Kim. *Enlightenment: Discovering the World in the Eighteenth Century.* London: The British Museum Press, 2003.
Supreme Grand Chapter of Royal Arch Masons of England. *History of Supreme Grand Chapter.* 2005. http://www.grandchapter.org.uk/sgc/gcr-history.htm (accessed July 12, 2013).
The Library and Museum of Freemasonry. *Annual Returns 1745-1814*. 2013. http://www.nationalarchives.gov.uk/a2a/records.aspx?cat=1991-ar_2&cid=-1#-1 (accessed August 11, 2013).
—. *Catalogue.* July 2013. http://www.freemasonry.london.museum/catalogue.php (accessed July/August 2013).
—. *Meeting in a Bottle.* 1 July 2004. http://www.freemasonry.london.museum/showcase/meeting-in-a-bottle/ (accessed August 2, 2013).
United Grand Lodge of England. "General Laws and Regulations for the Government of the Craft." *United Grand Lodge Book of Constitutions.* December 1813. http://www.ugle.org.uk/images/files/Book_of_Constitutions_-_Craft_rev_9.pdf (accessed July 12, 2013).
—. *Masonic Offering to His Royal Highness Prince Augustus Frederick, Duke of Sussex KG etc., etc., etc., Grand Master of the Freemasons in England.* London: Norris and Son, 1838.
—. *What is Freemasonry?* 2012-13. http://www.ugle.org.uk/what-is-freemasonry (accessed August 1, 2013).

INDEX